Differentiating Assessment
in the Writing Workshop

Karin Ma & Nicole Taylor

New York • Toronto • London • Auckland • Sydney
Mexico City • New Delhi • Hong Kong • Buenos Aires

Teaching *Resources*

To my best friend, Bishop, with love.

-KM

To the greatest inspiration in my life.
Sanáa, Mommy loves you!
Thanks for helping with the book.

-NT

Editor: Sarah Longhi
Content editing: Sarah Glasscock
Cover design: Brian La Rossa
Interior design: Kelli Thompson
Illustrations: Maxi Chambliss

ISBN-13: 978-0-545-05398-3
ISBN-10: 0-545-05398-6

1 2 3 4 5 6 7 8 9 10   40   15 14 13 12 11 10 09

Contents

All reproducible forms are available on
the companion CD

Introduction

Conferring—Unlocking the Power of Assessment

"I think we've complicated the idea of conferring. Teachers need to see that they've been conferring their whole lives. They need to recall moments when they've been good listeners and moments when they've helped someone see options, make decisions, and take risks. Of course, conferring about writing is usually not that simple. But we have to begin with the belief that we can do it, that indeed, we've been doing it well for years."

SHELLEY HARWAYNE, (1992) *LASTING IMPRESSIONS*

Conferring appears to be an arduous task, but it doesn't have to be. As teachers, we talk to our students all day long in an effort to guide them on the path to success. By adding some structure to these interactions we can make our work with students even more effective. And when we create a system like the one we present in this book, with clear procedures for conferring and maintaining accurate and detailed assessment notes, we are able to better assist our students and ensure that their writing reaches its full potential.

Listed below are some of the many questions we've heard from teachers about conferring.

- How will I be able to meet with so many students?
- When can I make time to meet with my students?
- What do I say?
- What should I teach them now?
- How do I organize my notes—and what do I do with them?
- What will my other students do while I'm conferring?
- How can I make sure students will follow through on the skills I have taught them?
- How can I differentiate conferences to meet all my students' needs?
- How can I use these notes to communicate with the school community?
- Why should I confer anyway?

All of these questions will be addressed in the upcoming chapters, with the aim of helping you put this new assessment system into practice in your own classroom.

How This Book Developed

We met as new kindergarten teachers in the fall of 2001 as we were about to embark on the school year in a brand new school in New York City. The moment we met, we formed an instant bond. We had similar teaching styles, the same enthusiasm for learning, and high expectations for ourselves and our students. We quickly discovered how difficult managing a primary classroom is—in addition to planning a reading and writing curriculum that met and challenged all students. To support one another, we met frequently outside of the classroom to share what we were teaching and plan for the upcoming months. We still maintain this practice today.

A few summers ago, we thought to ourselves, "How about developing a system of conferring that could really work in the classroom?" We had tried several different conferring systems in the past, but none ever worked as we had envisioned. Some of our first systems for taking notes involved many sheets of loose-leaf paper that were frequently lost, as well as notes jotted haphazardly in notebooks that we never looked at again. We even tried using sticker labels that we were supposed to make notes on during the writing workshop and then transfer over to student record sheets. After a couple of months, these stickers ended up staying right where we left them. Everything was time-consuming and inefficient. We felt that our students deserved more, and so did we. Why confer at all if it wasn't helping us plan instruction and improve student work?

We wanted to develop a system for conferring that would enable us to take notes quickly so we could spend more time teaching. It was always difficult to decide quickly what deserved a compliment and which skills to teach students. We thought that having a reference at the top of our conference notes showing the skills we expected students to master during the unit would help us decide what to say during a conference. By thinking ahead of time about unit goals and objectives, we would have a better plan for each individual conference. We could even differentiate for each writer's needs.

Our Writing Conference Notes sheets helped us develop the method that we've come to depend on—assessment, planning, and instruction through conferring. By creating a conference note sheet for each unit, we realized we could track lesson and unit goals. Everything we needed for writing conferences and even small group work would be right there on the sheet. It would take the guesswork out of conferring, and it was a simple, yet effective way to confer!

Standards-Based Instruction and Conferring

When we began to implement the writing workshop model in our classrooms, we quickly realized that we could easily help our students meet—and often exceed—all the city and state standards through this approach to instruction. The inclusion of these standards—at each grade level—is a cornerstone of each unit of study that helps us to differentiate instruction and assessment.

The following is an overview of the New York State literacy standards and how we align them with our writing instruction:

• **Standard 1 requires students to write for information and understanding.** According to the standard, "they will use oral and written language to acquire, interpret, apply, and transmit information." Through studying and writing nonfiction pieces, students are able to accomplish this goal.

• **Standard 2 requires that students should write "for self-expression and artistic creation."** Throughout the year, students are able to choose their own topics and generate story ideas. They create characters and plot lines for realistic fiction and express themselves through poetry.

● **Standard 3 requires that students "will present, in oral and written language and from a variety of perspectives, their opinions and judgments on experiences, ideas, information and issues."** Students utilize share time to evaluate each other's work, as well as use writing partners during the units. Editing helps students to analyze their work for grammar, spelling, and punctuation errors.

● **Standard 4 requires that "students will use oral and written language for effective social communication with a wide variety of people."** Throughout the year, students write for a purpose and learn that their writing will be read. They consider their audience, and look forward to sharing their work.

With careful planning, the writing workshop helps us to maintain standards-based instruction. From this planning work, we help you take efficient and purposeful conference notes to keep track of how well your students are progressing toward meeting these standards and to differentiate your planning in light of these assessments.

How to Use This Book

Throughout this book, you will explore different scenarios you may have encountered in your own classroom. These scenarios will prepare you for anything you might face the next time you confer. Sample conferences, mini-lessons, and strategy group lessons are sprinkled throughout the chapters to help you picture what your workshop might look and sound like. Writing Conference Notes sheets are filled in to showcase how this new system of conferring can work for you. Although every classroom is unique and there are so many different kinds of students, we attempted to help you differentiate your instruction to help meet all of their needs. For instance, we've included English language learner (ELL) tips throughout this book. Here is how the book is laid out.

Chapter 1 offers an overview of conferring. You will gain insight into the parts of a conference, how conferring can be a useful assessment tool in your classroom, when you should do it, and how to stay organized.

Chapter 2 explains exactly how to take conference notes effectively and efficiently to collect exactly the data you need. We suggest several options for how to take notes so you can choose which way works best for you. Common concerns about how to organize and manage your new assessment system will be addressed.

In **Chapter 3**, we show you how conferring fits into ten units of study that we use each year to cover our curriculum and meet state literacy standards. You can decide which units you'd like to teach—or how to adapt our ideas to your own units—and when to teach them. You will come across many writing samples for grades K–2 so you can see how authentic conferences help support a primary writing curriculum. These samples highlight ongoing work as well as published pieces. They reflect students of varying abilities as well as children learning the English language. Sample conference note sheets help you visualize what the system will look like when you begin to use it. We provide examples of literature we love to use during these units, as well as different celebrations we've successfully tried in the past.

Chapter 4 provides portraits of students at differing ability levels. We closely examine students who are writing at, below, and above grade-level expectations in grades K–2 and paint a picture of how these children are likely to begin the school year. This will help you get started with the writing workshop, and help you know what to expect and the best way to reach students during conferring time. Student writing samples and conference note sheet samples help illustrate these expectations.

The strategies in **Chapter 5** give teachers a better grasp of organization and planning. Conference notes are sometimes difficult to compile and look at collectively, so this chapter shows how to use checklists to inform your future instruction, whether it's individual, small-group, or whole-class.

Chapter 6 discusses how to use assessment data from your conferences to better communicate within your school community about student progress. Improving communication with parents, teachers, administrators, as well as students, will ensure children's progress continues throughout the school year. Utilizing your conference notes sheets effectively can help you convey any concerns you have for students within your classroom.

How to Use the Companion CD

Like most teachers, we love to get tools that help simplify our lives. We wanted to make sure our readers would have the tools they needed to implement this method of taking conference notes. The companion CD contains customizable versions of all the conferring and planning forms shown in this book, which are also available as reproducible pages in the Appendix (pages 106–143). In this way, you may photocopy the reproducible form or print it from the CD and fill it in by hand, or you may fill in the digital form, print it, and save the digital file to update—in fact, you may want to make an assessment folder on your hard drive for each child. You can record your students' names, the date, and quick, targeted notes that will become an organized part of each student's record.

The ideas and tools presented in this book will help ensure your success this school year and in the future. You will feel much more confident about your ability to maintain assessment records and to use them to make instructional decisions in your classroom.

Tip

To customize and save the files on the CD, you will need to download Adobe Reader™, version 7.0 or higher. This download is available free of charge for Mac and PC systems at www.adobe.com/products/acrobat/readstep2.

Chapter 1

Conferring 101: Basic Tools to Make Assessment Work

"[Conferences] are not mini-lectures but the working talk of fellow writers sharing their experience with the writing process."

DONALD M. MURRAY, (2003) *A WRITER TEACHES WRITING*

As a teacher, you want to portray yourself as a writer. You maintain your own writing folder, produce grade-appropriate writing samples to show students, and publish your own piece of writing along with theirs. The students come to view you as a fellow writer—and not simply as a writing teacher. The most important aspect of this relationship is the conversation that happens between two writers. This trust that develops will help you confer effectively within your classroom and take quality assessment notes.

In this chapter you'll learn about the following topics:

- What are the parts of a conference?
- How should I decide what to teach the writers in my class?
- How can conferencing help me as a teacher?
- What's the best time to confer?
- Where should I conference?
- How can I use writing partners effectively?
- How can I stay organized?

How Is a Conference a Conversation?

At the start of the school year, you want to create an inviting tone so your students feel like they are active participants in the conferences you have with them. Conversations require that at least two people speak, and that back-and-forth dialogue is what you want to start in September.

Productive conversations imply that you are a great listener, and that skill starts with you, the teacher. By listening closely to what your young writers have to say, you can identify and research their needs, and begin the important assessment work that is conferring. A conference is a tool that teachers can use to help assess their students and inform their instruction. Research is one of the most important parts of conferring. It requires that teachers step back and look to see what their class is doing to first determine what individual students might need.

In the following example, you'll see how Ms. D, a kindergarten teacher, uses frequent conferences with her students.

September has just begun and K-105 is learning the routines of writing workshop from Ms. D. After her lesson is complete, Ms. D takes

Karin sits back and looks over the writing before making any decisions. This research helps guide her assessment.

a glance at all of the smiling faces of her kindergarten class. She takes a deep breath and sends the children off to begin writing workshop. She grabs her conferring notebook and looks at her conference checklist (see a description and example of this form on page 23). "Which writers haven't I met with in a while?" she thinks to herself. Mary, Billy, and José don't have a check next to their names yet. Which one should she meet with first? Ms. D. scans the classroom to see how each student is doing and notices that Mary is off-task. She decides to confer with her first.

Ms. D is an educator who plans well. She knows there are many goals kindergarteners must achieve in order for a writing workshop to run successfully and smoothly, so she begins the school year with lessons that set the tone for the rest of students' writing lives. She also follows up these lessons with conferences to support the writers further and help them reach their goals.

Ms. D gains key insight into which student to meet with first when she takes a few moments to look around the room and at her conferring notebook. She takes out a new Writing Conference Notes sheet and writes Mary's name on it. Watch closely as she begins her conference with Mary.

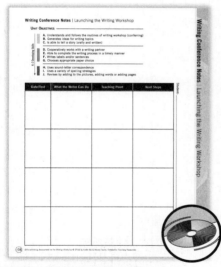

Writing Conference Notes Sheet
Print From CD/Copy From
Appendix, page 107
(Find reproducible conference note sheets for ten units of study and a blank template, pages 107–117)

Ms. D: Mary, what are you working on today?

Mary: Nothing.

Ms. D: Let's take a look at your writing. Can you show me your writing?

Mary: Okay!

(Mary opens her writing folder and hands Ms. D her writing piece. There is an illustration that doesn't seem complete. There are no words on the page.)

Ms. D: Mary, what is your writing about?

Mary: Mommy and me at the park.

(Ms. D points to the picture.)

Ms. D: Show me.

Mary: That's mommy.

Ms. D: I see!

Ms. D completes her research, which consists of looking at what Mary is doing, speaking with her about her writing, and examining her piece of writing. Now it's time to give Mary a compliment and decide what to teach her next. Ms. D looks over her notes and picks one thing to compliment her on.

Ms. D: Wow Mary! It's so smart that you drew the character for your story in the picture. Mommy must be very important to your story!

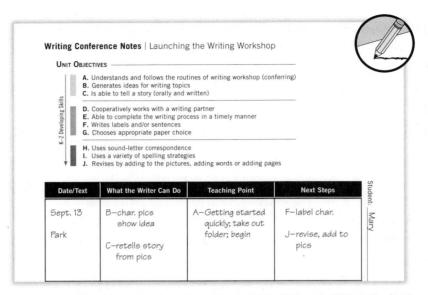

Writing Conference Notes | Launching the Writing Workshop

UNIT OBJECTIVES

K-2 Developing Skills

A. Understands and follows the routines of writing workshop (conferring)
B. Generates ideas for writing topics
C. Is able to tell a story (orally and written)

D. Cooperatively works with a writing partner
E. Able to complete the writing process in a timely manner
F. Writes labels and/or sentences
G. Chooses appropriate paper choice

H. Uses sound-letter correspondence
I. Uses a variety of spelling strategies
J. Revises by adding to the pictures, adding words or adding pages

Date/Text	What the Writer Can Do	Teaching Point	Next Steps
Sept. 13 Park	B—char. pics show idea C—retells story from pics	A—Getting started quickly; take out folder; begin	F—label char. J—revise, add to pics

Student: Mary

Ms. D jots down what she notices Mary can do in the "What the Writer Can Do" column of the Writing Conferences Notes sheet. As the conference progresses, she adds notes about her teaching point and possible next steps for Mary.

Ms. D has been thinking about all of the possible teaching points for this conference. She glances at the unit's objectives on the conferring sheet. Through her research, Ms. D decides that Mary needs help with (A) following the routines, (F) labeling the characters in the picture, and (J) revising by adding to the picture. After prioritizing, she decides to work on (A) following the routines with Mary. As a veteran teacher, she knows how imperative it is to get the routines set before working on anything else with a student. Ms. D jots down her teaching point and possible next steps before continuing the conference. Then she resumes with her target teaching point.

Ms. D: Mary, I want to teach you something so that you can become an even better writer. It's important for writers to get started right away when it's writing time. As soon as I send you off to write, I want you to take your writing out of your folder and begin. Watch me with my folder. You can pretend to be the teacher. What would I say?

Mary: Boys and girls, go off to write!

(Ms. D takes her out of her folder, thinks aloud for a few seconds about what she will write today, and then begins to write.)

Ms. D: Did you see what I just did Mary? I got my writing out of my folder and started right away. Now you try it.

(Mary takes her writing out of her folder and begins to add to her picture.)

Ms. D: So every time I send the class to begin writing, I want to see you taking your writing out of your folder so that you can start right away.

As you see, Ms. D completes her conference with her teaching point. She clearly states what she wants Mary to do. Then she models the teaching point and directs Mary to try it herself. Ms. D reminds her of the teaching point again before she ends the conference.

The Parts of an Effective Conference

Most conferences that you have will sound similar to the one Ms. D had with Mary. You begin by researching the class and student, deciding what the student does well, complimenting him or her, deciding on your teaching point, and teaching a specific unit objective. Always remember to restate the teaching point throughout the conference to ensure your students will know what to do. Use consistent language in your mini-lessons as well as in your conferences. Choose your words wisely. Think: *Will my students understand what I mean?* The conference note sheet will help you figure out which goal to focus on. It's also a great way to keep track of your conference.

Getting to Know Your Writers: Early Assessments

Conferences help you get to know your students well. In September, you may also want to give students a "Meet Our Writers" interview sheet to help you get a better picture of the kinds of writers in your classroom. We've included an interview sheet for levels K–1 (top right) and a more advanced one for levels 1–2 (bottom right).

The K–1 interview sheet at right can be given to your youngest writers. The picture support will help them fill it out. You may also want to send the sheet home so parents can help their child fill it out.

The 1–2 sheet provides even more information about the writers in your classroom. Gifted first graders and second-grade students benefit from filling out this detailed interview sheet. You might even pair the writers in your classroom and have them interview one another. They can work on their listening and questioning skills while getting to know one another at the start of the school year. Sheets like these help build the writing community in your classroom.

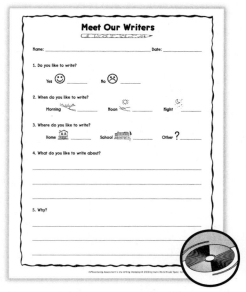

Meet Our Writers K–1 Interview Sheet
Print From CD/Copy From Appendix, page 133

Meet Our Writers 1–2 Interview Sheet
Print From CD/Copy From Appendix, page 134

Why Confer?

Conferring is at the heart of the writing workshop. It provides insight into your students' present success while informing your future instruction. Praise is a powerful motivator for any child. The compliments you give during conferences make children feel confident in their abilities as writers. Because children are often unaware of the crafts they use when writing, it is important to confer so you can build student confidence as well as provide assessment-based instruction to everyone.

ASSESSMENT AS A MOTIVATOR

As a teacher, you strive to meet the individual needs of all your students. Conferences can be a special time of the day for you to get to know your children. They come to expect your help and look forward to the next conference. Taking time to speak with each child lets them know that they are important to you. This helps build a special community in your classroom. Children gain the necessary confidence to succeed in this risk-free environment. They become confident writers.

The following example shows how a first-grade teacher, Mr. L, effectively uses conferring to motivate his students.

It's November in Mr. L's first-grade class. Students are actively writing during writing workshop time now that they have mastered basic routines. Mr. L glances over at Samuel's piece of writing. He notices the illustration has some important details to help tell the story. Samuel has labeled the characters in his writing, as Mr. L previously instructed. To his pleasant surprise, Mr. L notices the mom in the picture is smiling. He compliments Samuel for showing feeling by adding facial expressions. Samuel beams with pride.

Nicole's | Classroom Notes

Every year, there are several shy children in my classroom. These children never seem to want to share their work with the whole class. The idea of standing in front of all the student writers is scary. I like to give these students the opportunity to feel pride, just like everyone else. One way I have successfully dealt with this is by sharing their writing for them. I give a child the option by asking, "Would you like to read your piece or should I?" Usually, these shy writers love it when I read their pieces aloud. The other writers give compliments that encourage these little authors to continue to write!

At share time, Mr. L restates the compliment and allows Samuel to show the class what he's done. Later that week, Mr. L peruses the students' writing folders and is pleasantly surprised again. He notices several children have now added facial expressions to their character illustrations. He realizes what a powerful motivator compliments can be.

ASSESSMENT DRIVES INSTRUCTION

Your assessment of each student will help you make future instructional decisions. Conference notes become a useful guide to lesson planning within your classroom. When you confer again with a student, it's helpful to glance at your notes before making any decisions. Looking back at a previously noted teaching point is the starting point for your research.

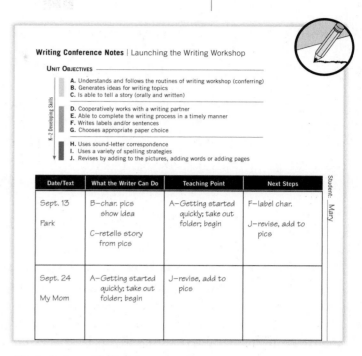

Writing Conference Notes | Launching the Writing Workshop

UNIT OBJECTIVES

K–2 Developing Skills

A. Understands and follows the routines of writing workshop (conferring)
B. Generates ideas for writing topics
C. Is able to tell a story (orally and written)

D. Cooperatively works with a writing partner
E. Able to complete the writing process in a timely manner
F. Writes labels and/or sentences
G. Chooses appropriate paper choice

H. Uses sound-letter correspondence
I. Uses a variety of spelling strategies
J. Revises by adding to the pictures, adding words or adding pages

Student: Mary

Date/Text	What the Writer Can Do	Teaching Point	Next Steps
Sept. 13 Park	B—char. pics show idea C—retells story from pics	A—Getting started quickly; take out folder; begin	F—label char. J—revise, add to pics
Sept. 24 My Mom	A—Getting started quickly; take out folder; begin	J—revise, add to pics	

Ms. D confers with Mary on a new story

Listen in as Ms. D uses her notes effectively in another conference with Mary. She is able to use her previous assessment of the student to choose a new teaching point. Because Mary masters a skill that Ms. D has introduced to her earlier in the school year, (A) following the routines, Ms. D can choose a new skill to work on with Mary—clarifying her pictures with setting details. Note that the conversation below also illustrates how Ms. D turns the previous teaching point into a compliment when she notices that Mary is now able to get started right away. If Mary had not been able to do this, Ms. D would have retaught the objective. Based on her conference notes, Ms. D is able to differentiate instruction. This ensures that Mary will become a successful writer.

> **Ms. D:** Mary, I noticed that today you got started with your writing just like we spoke about. Good for you!
>
> (Ms. D looks over the Next Steps column to choose a new teaching point.)
>
> **Ms. D:** I'd like to teach you how you can make your pictures clearer by showing where you are in your story.
>
> (Ms. D asks Mary to read her story.)
>
> **Mary:** I went to the beach with my mommy.
>
> **Ms. D:** Oh boy! That sounds like fun! So you went to the beach with your mommy? What kinds of things did you see at the beach?
>
> **Mary:** I saw lots of water and sand. It was so hot!

Ms. D: Today you can add all those things in your picture so that we know where you are in your story. You can add the hot sun, all that water from the ocean, and the sand all around you.

Conferring is an ongoing teaching and assessment tool that will benefit you and your students in so many ways. It helps create a climate of caring and responsibility in your classroom. Children know you will check to make sure they are following through on what you taught them to do, so they are held accountable for implementing these skills. As a result of your ongoing assessments, your students' writing will grow tremendously throughout the school year.

When to Confer?

Conferring is done daily after your writing workshop mini-lesson. (For more information on writing workshops, see Chapter 2.) Give students a few minutes to settle down. These precious moments also give you a chance to assess how successfully they are following the routines. Be sure to scan the room for behavioral concerns. What you notice will help you develop teaching points for future conferences. You may also want to take the time to look back at your conferring notes.

Karin's | Classroom Notes

When I have children who have difficulty settling into the writing period, I make sure I scan the room each day before beginning to confer. One quick glance at a child who is off task serves as a visual warning and quickly gets the child back on the right track. Addressing their behavioral concerns first allows me to focus on the unit objectives and get the most out of the writing period.

WHO NEEDS YOU THE MOST? PRIORITIZING YOUR CONFERENCE SCHEDULE

Conferences are crucial to your students' success, but they can be time-consuming. In order to meet with as many students as possible in a period, you will need to strategize, taking into account the different needs of your students.

If students are lagging behind in meeting the standards for promotion in the grade, they should become a priority in your conferring schedule.

Be sure to meet with these children more frequently so that you have many assessments on them and feel prepared to meet with parents and administrators to discuss student progress at a moment's notice. English language learners may also need to meet with you more frequently to ensure their writing stays on course. By keeping meticulous conference notes on these student writers, you will have the knowledge you need to help them make strides during the school year.

As you become more comfortable using conferring notes, your conference time will get cut in half. You will discover the most effective ways to take notes and how to use your previous assessments quickly to help you decide what to teach, which will give you time to meet with more students. An average conference should take approximately five to eight minutes.

Scheduling the Writing Workshop in Your School Day

There are several times in a day when you might plan your writing workshop. This important decision determines when you will conduct your writing assessments. You want to make the most out of your conferring time, so choosing a time of day that works for your classroom is crucial. Take a close look at your individual class to see what part of the day works best for you.

When children walk in first thing in the morning, they are alert and may have lots of writing ideas. Children are natural storytellers and are eager to share their stories. Morning workshops can also help settle the class down. After lunch or after recess can be opportune times for writing workshops as well. Writing tends to be a calming activity and allows children time to wind down. Many of our students' story ideas have been inspired by recess.

Our | Classroom Notes

Holding writing workshop after lunch works best for us. For the first ten minutes, we allow the children to use the bathroom and get drinks. Meanwhile, we put on some relaxing music, such as Enya or Mozart, which creates a calm setting for writing time. This settling-down period provides a great time for writers to reread their work and plan what writing they might do that day. We've found this period also encourages children to edit their work independently. We are able to make the most of bathroom time too! While children are working on their own or using the restroom, we take the opportunity to gather any materials we need for our mini-lessons. After children have settled down, we start our mini-lessons and set up the writing plans for the day.

Whatever time you choose, consistency is a key element. Children learn to expect writing workshop at that time of the day. They are more successful when a consistent schedule is followed.

FLEXIBLE SCHEDULING

You can choose to organize your conference schedule in many different ways. If you like to have complete control over which students you meet with on a regular basis, try assigning a conference schedule in which each table meets with you on a different day of the week. Posting a chart like the one below serves as a visual reminder to students. It also prevents them from constantly asking, "When are you conferring with me?"

When Will You Conference With Me? chart posted in classroom

These students are hard at work at their table while the teacher moves around the room to confer.

For more flexibility, you can choose on the spot which students to meet with. Moving around from table to table helps with management. This is especially useful for kindergarten and first-grade students. Your presence at a particular table often helps students stay on task.

In order to promote more independence in your writing workshop, you may want to create a conference sign-up sheet like the one shown on page 19. You will still have an opportunity to meet with students of your choosing while allowing for student ownership. It's more challenging to keep track of all the students in your class with this system, but students will usually keep you informed if their writing has gone astray. This kind of schedule works best with second-grade students or a mature first-grade class.

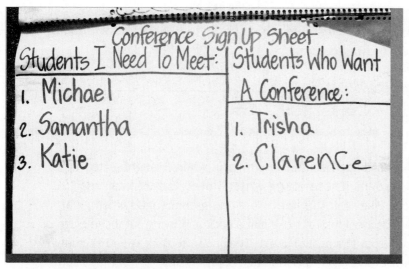

Conference Sign-Up Sheet posted in classroom

PEERS AS MENTOR WRITERS: A BUDDY SYSTEM THAT WORKS

How can you ensure that all of your students are successful with their writing pieces on a particular day, without meeting with each student? "Writing Buddies" is a great solution to this problem. As you confer with an individual child, students can take an active role in the conferring process with a peer.

Think carefully about how the buddy system will work effectively in your classroom. Students can be paired in several ways. When making partner decisions, consider student ability as well as personality. An outgoing student may be successfully paired with a quieter one. Sometimes writers who need more support may benefit from being paired with writers who are performing on grade level.

Writers who are ready for an additional challenge may work well together by supporting one another and exchanging ideas to improve the quality of their pieces. One important way these buddies can support each other is by using familiar

ELL Tip

English Language Learners [ELLs] are a special consideration in the classroom. Students who speak English proficiently can be paired with an ELL student so that he or she gets additional support. It is also a good idea to create a supportive buddy group involving three students so that the English Language Learner can hear native speakers in a comfortable group setting and will not feel pressured to communicate. Pairing up an ELL student with a proficient student who speaks her native language can also prove beneficial so that the ELL student can have an opportunity to get her ideas across in her own native language. The native speaker can also "confer" with the ELL student in a language she understands.

books that you have read aloud often to gain insights into their writing. These mentor texts model quality writing crafts that students hope to emulate in their own writing, and buddies can learn to assist each other with this process. They can look at mentor texts together and notice special crafts the writers have used successfully. Then students can try these crafts in their own pieces of writing. Peers can support each other by helping to determine which crafts to use and how to incorporate them in their writing pieces.

Nicole's | Classroom Notes

Mentor texts became very helpful when I taught gifted first graders. These young writers loved to feel like "real" authors. They felt that they were being challenged when given the independent task of looking at a book and trying out techniques or "crafts" that the author used. They soon took it upon themselves to name crafts, like repetition and sound words, which they found during independent reading and read-aloud time. Parents also found mentor texts helpful to use at home. These texts challenged their children and encouraged them to write stories at home. Choosing (or allowing students and parents to choose) authors whose work challenges and supports the writing students might attempt independently is one way I differentiate instruction.

Another great way to make the most of conference time is to have an intergrade buddy system. Upper-grade students are ready and able to help primary children with their writing. Their expertise can be especially useful during the editing phase of writing workshop. These young "editors-in-chief" will feel special knowing that their skills are valuable, and you will get much needed help through their conferring. Editing a piece chosen for publication takes only a few days in the classroom, and it is difficult to meet with all the children in that short time span. Using fourth- or fifth-grade buddies will ensure that all your students have effectively edited their work. These buddies can be brought into the classroom for a couple of days at the end of each month when your students are preparing their writing for publishing. Moreover, involving all students in the school in the writing process creates a supportive writing community.

Karin's | Classroom Notes

have found that writing buddies are useful not only during independent writing time but also at share time. I love to allow buddies to share their work at their seats at the end of the workshop. Partners usually ask specific questions because they're interested in their friend's story, and everyone has a chance to showcase his writing. When I hear writers ask sophisticated questions like "How did that make you feel?" I really get the sense that these young authors are helping each other.

Whatever buddy system you choose to implement in your classroom, it's important to create a chart showcasing which students are writing buddies. This will remind children of another person in the room who can help them when they are stumped during writing workshop. These buddies will learn how to confer with and assess one another, and can be an important component of the assessment system you've set up in your room.

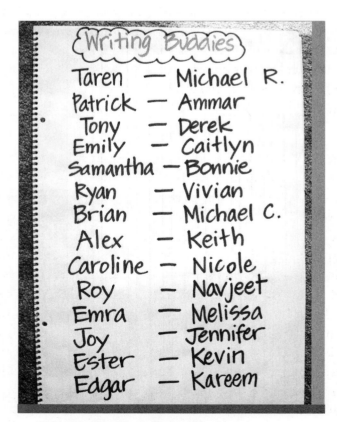

Writing Buddies chart displayed in classroom

Tools for Organizing and Preparing for Your Conferences

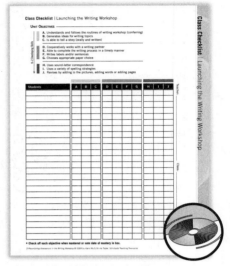

Class Checklist for Launching the Writing Workshop
Print From CD/Copy From Appendix, page 118
(Find reproducible checklists for ten units of study and a blank template, pages 118–128)

At first glance, taking and organizing your conference notes can seem overwhelming, but we've created some support forms to help you locate and organize information clearly. A Class Checklist sheet of the unit objectives helps to streamline and organize the data you've collected from your conference notes. On this form, you can see the ongoing progress of the class as a whole.

We include a Class Checklist sheet for each unit of study. The skills that students are expected to achieve by the end of the unit appear at the top of each checklist. Underneath the skills is a space to record which skills your students mastered.

There are many ways to successfully use these class checklist sheets. You may wish to check off the mastered skills directly after conferring with a student. This way the newly mastered skill is fresh in your mind. Another way is to look back at your conference note sheets on a weekly basis and fill in the newly mastered skills. Additionally, you can sort through student writing samples and check off any skills you see the students using. (Chapters 2 and 5 will give you a better picture of how to use these checklists in your classroom.)

Sample Class Checklist sheet for a second-grade class

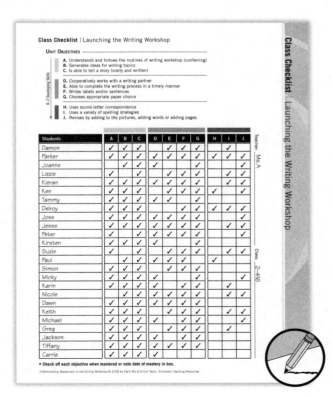

Class Checklist | Launching the Writing Workshop

UNIT OBJECTIVES

A. Understands and follows the routines of writing workshop (conferring)
B. Generates ideas for writing topics
C. Is able to tell a story (orally and written)

D. Cooperatively works with a writing partner
E. Able to complete the writing process in a timely manner
F. Writes labels and/or sentences
G. Chooses appropriate paper choice

H. Uses sound-letter correspondence
I. Uses a variety of spelling strategies
J. Revises by adding to the pictures, adding words or adding pages

Students	A	B	C	D	E	F	G	H	I	J
Damon	✓	✓	✓		✓	✓	✓		✓	
Parker	✓	✓	✓	✓	✓	✓	✓	✓	✓	✓
Joanne		✓	✓	✓			✓			✓
Lizzie	✓		✓		✓	✓	✓		✓	✓
Kieran	✓	✓	✓	✓	✓	✓	✓		✓	✓
Ken	✓	✓	✓		✓	✓	✓	✓		✓
Tammy	✓	✓	✓	✓	✓	✓				
Delroy	✓	✓	✓			✓	✓	✓	✓	✓
Jose	✓	✓	✓	✓	✓	✓	✓			✓
Jesse	✓	✓	✓	✓	✓	✓	✓		✓	✓
Peter	✓		✓	✓	✓	✓	✓			✓
Kirsten	✓	✓	✓			✓				
Suzie	✓				✓	✓	✓		✓	✓
Paul		✓	✓	✓	✓	✓		✓		
Simon	✓	✓	✓		✓	✓	✓			
Micky	✓	✓	✓	✓			✓			✓
Karin	✓	✓	✓				✓		✓	
Nicole		✓	✓	✓	✓	✓	✓		✓	✓
Dawn	✓	✓	✓	✓	✓	✓	✓			✓
Keith	✓	✓	✓		✓	✓	✓		✓	✓
Michael	✓	✓	✓	✓		✓	✓			✓
Greg	✓	✓	✓		✓	✓	✓		✓	
Jackson	✓	✓	✓	✓	✓	✓	✓			
Tiffany	✓	✓	✓	✓	✓	✓	✓			
Carrie	✓	✓	✓							

Teacher: Ms. A   Class: 2-416

* Check off each objective when mastered or note date of mastery in box.

Differentiating Assessment in the Writing Workshop © 2008 by Karin Ma & Nicole Taylor, Scholastic Teaching Resources

At a glance, the checklists provide you with insight into how you and your class are doing. The sample class checklist on page 22 from Ms. A's second-grade class shows you how it might look in the middle of the unit.

Having a record of student mastery helps you make smart teaching and assessment choices. In Ms. A's case, since most students in the class have a checkmark under skill B (generates ideas for writing topics), she no longer needs to reinforce this skill in future lessons—although she will continue to monitor and support Lizzie, Peter, and Suzie in individual conferences. When she realizes that most of her students do not have a check under objective H (uses sound/letter correspondence), Ms. A decides to create several mini-lessons supporting that skill. And she plans to pull a handful of children into a small-group strategy lesson to work on objective F (writes labels and/or sentences).

Because it can be difficult to ensure that you've met with every student several times during the course of a unit, we find that a Conference Dates Checklist is another good tool to use.

Using a simple list with students' names and spaces to check off every time you meet with these students helps ensure that you've met with every child before starting the cycle over. You may wish to record dates rather than use check marks so you know how long it has been since you've met with each student.

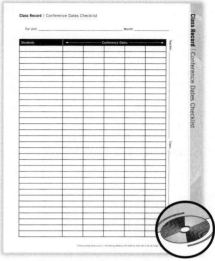

Conference Dates Class Checklist
Print From CD/Copy From Appendix, page 129

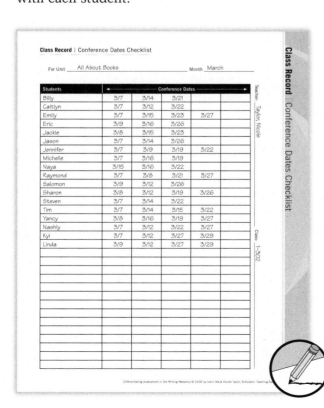

Class Record | Conference Dates Checklist

For Unit All About Books   Month March

Students	◄———	Conference Dates	———►	
Billy	3/7	3/14	3/21	
Caitlyn	3/7	3/12	3/22	
Emily	3/7	3/15	3/23	3/27
Eric	3/9	3/16	3/26	
Jackie	3/8	3/15	3/23	
Jason	3/7	3/14	3/26	
Jennifer	3/7	3/9	3/19	3/22
Michelle	3/7	3/16	3/19	
Naya	3/15	3/16	3/22	
Raymond	3/7	3/8	3/21	3/27
Salomon	3/9	3/12	3/26	
Sharon	3/8	3/12	3/19	3/26
Steven	3/7	3/14	3/22	
Tim	3/7	3/14	3/15	3/22
Yancy	3/8	3/16	3/19	3/27
Nashly	3/7	3/12	3/22	3/27
Kyi	3/7	3/12	3/27	3/29
Linda	3/9	3/12	3/27	3/29

Teacher Taylor, Nicole

Class 1-302

**Completed Conference Dates
Class Checklist for unit called
All About Books**

After a full week of conferring, you may feel as if you've met with the whole class, but sometimes this is not the case. Children may have been absent or away from their seat on the day you conferred with their table. Therefore, it's important to keep track of the students you confer with daily so you have weekly assessments on each child. This way, if Sammy was absent on Monday, the day of his conference, you'll notice a check missing beside his name at the end of the week, and make a mental note to meet with him another day. This list can also be enlarged and posted as a chart so that older children can put a check by their names after a conference. This will cut back some paperwork time for you.

Conferring is an important assessment tool in your classroom, and all your record-keeping sheets, including the individual conference note sheets and the class checklist sheets, will help you keep accurate, detailed, and informative assessment notes for each child in your classroom. It is up to you to decide how to implement this system in your classroom so that it best suits your students' needs. In the next chapter, we will take a closer look at how this system may work in your classroom and how it may fit within your writing workshop.

Chapter 2

How Is It All Done?

"The writing workshop follows the same structure as the independent reading workshop—it happens daily and begins with a mini-lesson followed by independent work time, and a teaching share time. During independent writing time, the children write or revise texts about self-selected topics while the teacher offers individual and small-group direct instruction during writing conferences and strategy lessons. During independent writing time, children have access to the materials they need to write, revise, edit, and publish the pieces they've written."

KATHY COLLINS, (2004) *GROWING READERS:*
UNITS OF STUDY IN THE PRIMARY CLASSROOM

nce you establish writing workshop in your classroom, you will see that it follows the same principles daily. The workshop becomes routine, and this routine helps keep the writers in your class on track. Your conferences will become short mini-lessons for individual students, and you will be able to differentiate your instruction so that all the writers in your classroom can succeed. Again, your conference notes will help you differentiate effectively.

In this chapter you will find out more about the following questions:
- How does conferring fit within the workshop model?
- How are a mini-lesson and a conference similar?
- How can I begin to confer for the school year?
- How do I take my conference notes?
- What are some common problems I might encounter?
- How can I solve these problems?

Conferring in the Writing Workshop Model

We follow a basic workshop model in which conferring is one of three components:
1. Mini-lesson
2. Conferring/small-group work
3. Share time

Every writing workshop starts with a mini-lesson, and then students go off to write independently. During independent writing, you have the opportunity to differentiate instruction by either conferring on an individual basis or conducting a small-group strategy lesson. Writing workshop concludes with a share time.

The Mini-Lesson

Since the mini-lesson often sets the tone and provides skill and strategy tips that you will use in a conference—and because the mini-lesson structure is similar to the conference structure—it's useful to review how it works. Every mini-lesson begins with a connection that sets a purpose for the writing that day. This may be a reminder or a compliment about students' past writing achievements. Next you teach the writing goal. This can be done in several ways. You can show examples, demonstrate, have students model (fishbowl-style), or use texts.

Teachers who show their own work samples motivate students to do a great job in their own writing.

After teaching the writing goal, you invite students to actively engage with pencil and paper or through peer discussion to try the skill or strategy right there on the rug, before they go off to work independently. Young writers can then make future plans for their writing pieces. The mini-lesson ends with a link to the writing time: a reminder of the teaching point.

There are many kinds of learners in every classroom, and it's important to consider ways to appeal to a range of learning styles when students are actively engaged in applying a new skill or strategy. (You should try out a variety of active engagement tactics during your conferences. Looking over past assessments of the children in your classroom, will give you a good picture of the kind of learners you are conferring with. This information enables you to differentiate the active engagement tactics to meet students' needs, as well as to keep each child interested and engaged.)

One mini-lesson can turn out in so many different ways, depending on the way you choose to differentiate. For instance, as you begin a new unit on nonfiction writing, you might start with a lesson teaching children to choose topics they know a lot about. The active engagement portion of this lesson might look different in different classrooms.

It's important to provide young writers time to try out the taught skill in their own writing. Be sure to have students bring their writing folders with them to the rug sometimes.

Charts with pictures serve as support for your visual learners. This chart reminds children how to tell their story sequentially across pages.

During active engagement time, these students are turning the pages in their own writing pieces to help them plan their writing for the day.

For visual learners, you might have children picture three things they know a lot about. Tactile learners benefit from touching and looking through books to give them ideas. (For more information about how to plan your lessons in a variety of ways, see Chapter 5. Also check out the Mini-Lesson Planning Sheet in the Appendix, page 129.)

Auditory learners can turn and talk to share their ideas, and sensory learners often find that acting out three things they can do very well is useful. For instance, children can act out skating or swimming or reading. One of these can then turn into an "All About" book on the topic.

A Mini-Lesson in Action

Mr. G begins a mini-lesson by modeling how to complete a "What's on my mind?" sheet.

Mr. G: Today I'm going to teach you that good writers get writing ideas from what's on their mind. What do we all have up here? (Mr. G. enthusiastically touches the top of his head.) A brain! Writers look inside their brain to get ideas. Look at the special paper I can use to show all the things that are on my mind. Watch how I take a minute to think about things that are on my mind.

Hmm... I've been thinking about all the fun things I do with my friends. And I've also been thinking an awful lot about my dog, Apollo. I can add that to my brain. Now... let's see! I've been thinking about all the great places I've been to on my bicycle. Let me put that right there on this side of my brain. (Mr. G models writing "friends," "my dog Apollo," and "bicycle" on the "What's on my mind?" sheet.) Do you writers see how I thought of different things that have been on my mind? Now I want you to think of two things that are going on in your mind. Turn and tell your partner.

(Mr. G monitors the different conversations in the classroom.)

Mr. G: I heard Peter tell Samuel that karate lessons are on his mind. I bet he's going to draw karate lessons on his brain. And Evelyn was telling Stephanie that her trip to Disney is on her mind. Today she'll add that to her brain. So, boys and girls, remember that today you'll add the things that have been on your mind to your paper. Now when you're stuck and don't know what to write, you can look at what's on your mind.

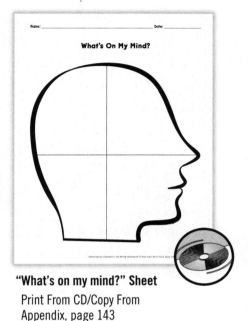

"What's on my mind?" Sheet
Print From CD/Copy From
Appendix, page 143

CONFERRING/SMALL-GROUP WORK

After the whole-class mini-lesson ends, students are sent to write on their own while the teacher differentiates instruction further through conferences and small-group work.

Children will write independently for varying amounts of time based on their age as well as the time of year. While students do this, you will have an opportunity to take out your conference note sheets and begin individual conferences or small-group instruction. Once again, consulting your writing conference notes will help you to differentiate your lessons. Keep in mind that the conference or small-group lesson follows the structure of the whole-class mini-lesson. The teacher chooses a skill for the children to work on, demonstrates it, and then has them try to use that skill in their writing.

SHARE TIME

The end of the writing workshop is signaled by share time. This is a great opportunity for students to be held accountable for the individualized instruction you provided during your conferences. By setting up the expectation that students need to follow through on the goal you set for them during your conferences, you're also teaching them that only students who continue to work on achieving their personalized goals will have an opportunity to share their writing with the whole class. Since students are usually very eager to share their writing, this is a good reward for the hard work they do as result of your conferences with them.

You can organize share time in many ways. You may invite writers to volunteer to read their pieces and showcase their successes based on your conferences with them, or you can choose to share specific work that highlights your lesson or "author crafts" you hope children will try in the future. Another option is to have all of your students

The teacher restates how Matthew followed through on his writing plan to revise his piece. Sharing this will encourage other students to do the same thing.

share what they tried through partnership time. Partners take turns reading aloud a piece of their work where they tried out the strategy you taught. This is a special time of the day that all children look forward to. The writers take pride in their accomplishments and often gain insights into future revision work. The class offers comments, questions, and suggestions regarding the pieces that are read aloud.

Our | Classroom Notes

We teach students how to respond to a friend's writing throughout the year. By reinforcing language frequently and providing children with prompts they might use, such as, "I like how you tried ..." the writers in our classrooms can be specific in their comments. This work truly shows itself when we have celebrations with parents and provide comment sheets like the one pictured below. Children begin to coach their parents and help them write comments that are clear. Rarely will we find a vague comment such as "Nice job!" Children love to read the compliments they've received and save their comments sheet after it's been filled in. We can even tell what students have learned during the course of the unit by looking at their comments.

Comment Sheet
Print From CD/Copy From Appendix, page 136

Conferring the Right Way

In order for conferring to run smoothly and be a success in your classroom, you need to set up a system that students understand and that is easy for you to use. It's important to start off the year right so you will have many opportunities for individualized instruction based on your student assessments. Below we show how Ms. C starts off her year.

It's the start of the second week of school, and writing workshop has been set in motion. Ms. C's first graders are enthusiastic about writing after she's talked it up so much in the first week of school. The students know how important writing is to Ms. C. It's her favorite time of the day. They've begun to follow the routines and rules without prompting during workshop time. Now Ms. C feels it's time for students to understand that she'll be conducting conferences and what they will be expected to do during a conference.

In addition to preparing a chart to go along with her lesson, she's also invited a former student, Sanáa, who is now in second grade, to come and help teach the first graders what a conference sounds like. Sanáa is excited to help out the new first graders learn the ropes. Inviting former students to show current students the structure of a conference is a useful strategy. Children tend to listen to other children, especially older students, and they will act out what they see. This strategy works for introducing children to peer conferring as well. Listen in as Ms. C begins her lesson on basic conference structure and procedures.

Ms. C: Boys and girls, we are so lucky to have a special expert in the room today to help us understand conferences a little better. Let's welcome Sanáa to class 110.

Class 110: Good morning Sanáa.

Ms. C: We've been learning all about how to start our writing. We have gotten to know where the supplies are located in the classroom. Today we are going to learn another part of writing workshop. Conferences are a special time for me to get to know you as a writer. Today I am going to teach you what you should do when I have a conference with you. Watch and notice what Sanáa does while I confer with her.

(Ms. C sets up her lesson for the class. She has spoken to Sanáa in advance to ensure that the lesson goes smoothly. Ms. C sits quietly next to Sanáa as she begins her writing. Ms. C takes a few moments to research the writer in front of her.)

Ms. C: What are you doing today, Sanáa, in your writing?

(Sanáa takes a minute to think and then looks over her work.)

Sanáa: Writing about Mommy and me at the park.

Ms. C: Can you read me your piece?

Sanáa: "I went to the park with my mommy. We went on the slide."

Ms. C: Wow! That must have been a fun day! I love how you remembered how to spell some sight words that you learned from kindergarten like *I*, *my*, and *the*. I want to give you an idea to help you with your writing today.

Sanáa: Great! Thanks!

Ms. C: I see you tried a couple of tricky words that you didn't know how to spell, like *park* and *slide*. When writers try to spell new words they say them three times and listen closely to the first sound or sounds they hear. Listen to me: "p-ark, p-ark, p-ark. I know! Park starts with a p." Now you try it.

(Sanáa says *slide* three times and records the correct initial sounds on her piece of paper.)

Ms. C: So remember … when you want to try to spell a word you don't know, you can say it three times and listen to the first sounds closely. Then write it down!

By showing your class what a great conference looks and sounds like, children will learn quickly what to do. Through this method, you've set the tone for your conferring for the rest of the year. Now Ms. C turns her attention to the children in her class.

Ms. C: Did everyone see what Sanáa and I did during our conference?

Class 110: Yes!

Ms. C: Take a minute to think about what you saw. Tell your neighbor two things we did well.

(The class quickly turns to talk to one another. Ms. C actively listens to several partners. She pulls out a chart like the one in the photo below to show the class some of the things they mention.)

Ms. C: Remember, I'm going to walk around and confer with several of you. If you forget what to do, you can look at the chart and remember what Sanáa did. Off you go to write.

As your students become experts at conferring, you can choose to take down the chart. Remember when making your own chart to use language that is commonplace in your classroom. Select words that you will use consistently and that you expect the children to use as well.

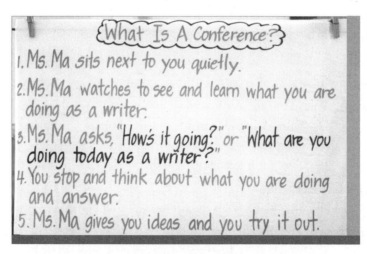

This chart is a good tool for students to refer to when they are not sure what to do.

This kind of mini-lesson is the best way to get your writing conferences started on the right track. Remember that students will need several reminders about routines and strategies they must practice independently, especially if they are not used to the workshop model.

Karin's | Classroom Notes

I always keep my charts simple. I make the sentences short and add a lot of picture support to help my first graders remember what the key words mean. I have a lot of English language learners in my classroom each year, and the pictures really help them understand the charts better. I often see children walk over to the charts and read them during workshop time. This helps them build greater independence and ownership of their work.

The pictures in this chart help students figure out different ways to start their stories and reminds them of vocabulary words taught, such as weather words.

Record Keeping

Your conference note sheets are a place for you to record helpful information for your future writing lessons and conferences. You'll notice in the example on page 34 that the specific unit objectives are listed clearly at the top of each sheet. Whether you choose to use the Writing Conference Note sheets we've included or to design your own, make sure that the unit objectives are listed accurately and reflect your goals and students' needs. The more familiar you are with the unit objectives, the more efficiently you are able to confer.

Tip

A blank Writing Conference Notes template is included on page 117 and on the CD. You may customize this form to reflect the goals of your own units of study.

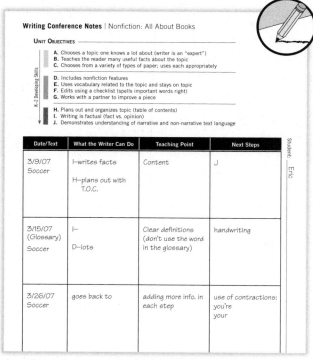

Writing Conference Notes | Nonfiction: All About Books

Unit Objectives

K–2 Developing Skills

A. Chooses a topic one knows a lot about (writer is an "expert")
B. Teaches the reader many useful facts about the topic
C. Chooses from a variety of types of paper; uses each appropriately

D. Includes nonfiction features
E. Uses vocabulary related to the topic and stays on topic
F. Edits using a checklist (spells important words right)
G. Works with a partner to improve a piece

H. Plans out and organizes topic (table of contents)
I. Writing is factual (fact vs. opinion)
J. Demonstrates understanding of narrative and non-narrative text language

Date/Text	What the Writer Can Do	Teaching Point	Next Steps
3/9/07 Soccer	I—writes facts H—plans out with T.O.C.	Content	J
3/15/07 (Glossary) Soccer	I— D—lots	Clear definitions (don't use the word in the glossary)	handwriting
3/26/07 Soccer	goes back to	adding more info. in each step	use of contractions: you're your

Student: Eric

Sample conference note sheet for an "All About Books" unit

Justin looks on as his teacher jots down her conferring notes.

Each time you meet with a student, be sure to record the date and the title/topic of the piece of writing. Comparing your notes from previous conferences will help you decide what you'd like to teach the writer. In the notes here, it's easy to see that Eric wrote about soccer each time the teacher met with him. If, for example, you've been working on writing many different personal narratives, and a writer is always stuck on the same topic, you may wish to teach him how to choose different ideas.

Next, record the skills that the student has mastered. Write a compliment you've given to the student under "What the Writer Can Do." After you've chosen an objective to teach, document it in the "Teaching Point" column. Record the objectives you'd like to delve into the next time you meet with the student under the "Next Steps" column.

Remember to make your notes short and concise. At first, you may wish to simply jot down the letter(s) that correspond to target objectives in the appropriate boxes. As you become more familiar with note taking, you may chose to write more elaborate notes. Keep in mind that the objectives at the top of the sheet list general goals you want your children to achieve. You may be more specific about the objective in your note taking, as shown in the top left example on page 35.

Here, the teacher uses letter symbols to note objectives C, D, and J, but she adds specific information to her notes as well. For example, on March 19, Sharon was able to include many nonfiction features (D). The teacher listed the features she used (diagram, zoom-in, table of contents, and heading).

To save time, you may choose to use shorthand as you make your notes (see top right example, page 35). It's helpful to have a system of abbreviations in place, such as between (btwn.), pictures (pics.), or questions (ques.). This system needs to work for you consistently and to feel natural.

Another quick and easy system for note taking is to check off or circle each objective when it's been mastered, as shown in the conference note sheet at the bottom of page 35.

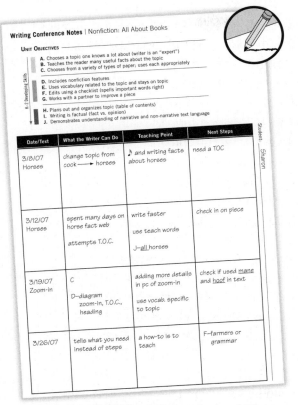

Writing Conference Notes | Nonfiction: All About Books

UNIT OBJECTIVES

K–2 Developing Skills

- A. Chooses a topic one knows a lot about (writer is an "expert")
- B. Teaches the reader many useful facts about the topic
- C. Chooses from a variety of types of paper; uses each appropriately

- D. Includes nonfiction features
- E. Uses vocabulary related to the topic and stays on topic
- F. Edits using a checklist (spells important words right)
- G. Works with a partner to improve a piece

- H. Plans out and organizes topic (table of contents)
- I. Writing is factual (fact vs. opinion)
- J. Demonstrates understanding of narrative and non-narrative text language

Student: Sharon

Date/Text	What the Writer Can Do	Teaching Point	Next Steps
3/8/07 Horses	change topic from cook → horses	♪ and writing facts about horses	need a TOC
3/12/07 Horses	spent many days on horse fact web attempts T.O.C.	write faster use teach words J–all horses	check in on piece
3/19/07 Zoom-in	C D–diagram zoom-in, T.O.C., heading	adding more details in pc of zoom-in use vocab. specific to topic	check if used mane and hoof in text
3/26/07	tells what you need instead of steps	a how-to is to teach	F–farmers or grammar

Your notes should be short, concise, readable—and understandable.

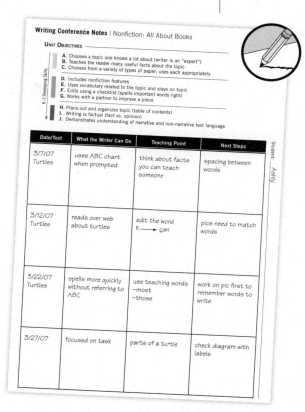

Writing Conference Notes | Nonfiction: All About Books

UNIT OBJECTIVES

K–2 Developing Skills

- A. Chooses a topic one knows a lot about (writer is an "expert")
- B. Teaches the reader many useful facts about the topic
- C. Chooses from a variety of types of paper; uses each appropriately

- D. Includes nonfiction features
- E. Uses vocabulary related to the topic and stays on topic
- F. Edits using a checklist (spells important words right)
- G. Works with a partner to improve a piece

- H. Plans out and organizes topic (table of contents)
- I. Writing is factual (fact vs. opinion)
- J. Demonstrates understanding of narrative and non-narrative text language

Student: Ashly

Date/Text	What the Writer Can Do	Teaching Point	Next Steps
3/7/07 Turtles	uses ABC chart when prompted	think about facts you can teach someone	spacing between words
3/12/07 Turtles	reads over web about turtles	edit the word K → can	pics need to match words
3/22/07 Turtles	spells more quickly without referring to ABC	use teaching words —most —those	work on pic first to remember words to write
3/27/07	focused on task	parts of a turtle	check diagram with labels

Using a consistent system of abbreviations can help speed your note taking.

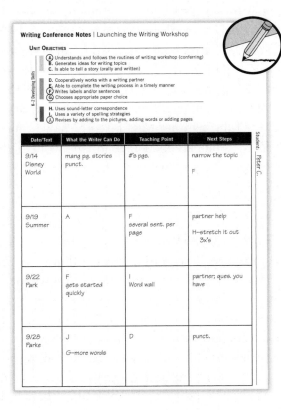

Writing Conference Notes | Launching the Writing Workshop

UNIT OBJECTIVES

K–2 Developing Skills

- A. Understands and follows the routines of writing workshop (conferring)
- B. Generates ideas for writing topics
- C. Is able to tell a story (orally and written)

- D. Cooperatively works with a writing partner
- E. Able to complete the writing process in a timely manner
- F. Writes labels and/or sentences
- G. Chooses appropriate paper choice

- H. Uses sound-letter correspondence
- I. Uses a variety of spelling strategies
- J. Revises by adding to the pictures, adding words or adding pages

Student: Peter C.

Date/Text	What the Writer Can Do	Teaching Point	Next Steps
9/14 Disney World	mang pg. stories punct.	#'s pgs.	narrow the topic F
9/19 Summer	A	F several sent. per page	partner help H–stretch it out 3x's
9/22 Park	F gets started quickly	I Word wall	partner; ques. you have
9/28 Parke	J G–more words	D	punct.

Circling mastered objectives can give you a quick overview of a student's progress.

A quick look at the top of the conference note sheet will give you a good indication of how the student is doing in the unit. If all the objectives are circled or checked off, mastery is complete and enrichment is an option. Your goal is to guide all students toward mastery by the end of the unit. If nothing is circled or checked off by mid-unit, extra attention should be given to this student. More information about how to use your notes to help you support remediation or enrichment of a particular skill appears in Chapters 4 and 5

Nicole's | Classroom Notes

When I work with gifted children, I often find that these students have already mastered most of the grade-level objectives early in the unit. They remember strategies that I taught in previous units and continue to apply them to their current work. This allows me to teach more challenging strategies, such as revision skills, I might otherwise have taught later in the year. I sometimes allow children to publish an extra piece that they work on with more independence.

For example, during our nonfiction unit, I had children publish an "All About" book about a favorite topic they had read about, followed by a research-based topic. During the first piece of writing, they didn't do any research, but rather learned how a nonfiction book should be written, as well as different features they could include. For their next nonfiction piece, they were able to transfer the skills that I had taught before about nonfiction conventions and features to their writing and they added new information about their topic by applying research skills I had recently introduced. This helped encourage independence and provided the students with a needed challenge.

COMPILING YOUR CONFERENCE NOTES

There are many ways you may choose to compile all your conference notes. For instance, you may print out sheets that correspond to the number of students in your class, and bind them into a conferring notebook.

A more compact and portable way to organize your notes is to assemble them into a three-ringed folder, with each unit kept in its own folder.

Management

Well-designed management is crucial to the success of any conferring system. Children need to learn what is expected of them during independent writing time so they can rise to the challenge of writing on their own. Starting in September you'll need to have a clear system of routines in place, including the following:

- How to keep students on task
- What to do while the teacher is conferring
- How to get help when the teacher in conferring
- Where to confer
- How to keep your conferring materials accessible

It is important to teach children how to work independently. Visual signals help remind students of what they need to do. At the start of the school year, many children will attempt to interrupt your conferences. One way to prevent this from happening is to wear a conference necklace with a note or picture that indicates you're busy. Anytime a child comes near hold it up as a reminder that you cannot help him or her at that moment. Another way to manage your students is to hold up a stop sign. Students will quickly learn this means "Stop, think, and go back to work." Students also need to learn that there are other teachers in the room—all of their peers. Wearing or posting a sign that reads, "Three before me!" tells children that they are responsible for themselves: They should ask three students for help before coming to you. It is imperative that students refrain from interrupting conference time. Early in the year, teach hand signals for bathroom and water breaks, such as a thumbs-up.

Our | Classroom Notes

We usually take the first month of school to continuously reinforce the management aspect of writing workshop. Consistency has been the key to our success. We show children how important uninterrupted conferring time is for us and, as the month of September comes to an end, the number of interruptions decreases dramatically. When visitors walk into our classrooms, they often ask, "How did you get the children so quiet?" Our answer is always the same: "Consistency." We have taught them our expectations during writing workshop, and students know that means they should be working quietly the whole time, without interrupting us. We and the writers in our classroom are so engaged in what we are doing that we often don't even notice when a visitor has entered our room.

Another aspect of management is where to conduct your conference. A conference corner (shown below) can be a place in the room where students come to meet with you. The advantages of having this nook are that you can store your materials in a central location and you can stay in one place rather than walking around the room. This often saves time.

This conferring nook allows the teacher to stay in one spot with all the assessment tools.

On the other hand, moving from table to table lets children know you are nearby, and your presence may help prevent behavioral problems. So you may opt for a conference stool that is easy to carry around. Another benefit of having a portable seat is that you can deliver teaching to the other students at the table where you hold a conference. While you are conferring with one student, all the children at the table can benefit from listening in on your conferences. This way, you will reach many more children during the writing period.

It is important to have all of your conferring materials handy.

A conference caddy like the one shown here can contain your conference notes, mentor texts, a well-organized model writing folder or a model writer's notebook (depending on which tool your students use), a record of shared writing that was created by the whole class, and model student writing samples. If you laminate these writing samples, you can highlight a writing skill on the spot using water-based markers, which you can erase after each use.

A conference caddy helps to keep you organized while you conduct your assessments.

White boards are great for illustrating your teaching point to students. You can use them to model what you want your students to try out in their writing.

By designing a system for your conferences, your students will know what you expect of them, and they will behave accordingly. It's important to think about all the aspects of management discussed above before the school year begins so you can begin immediately to teach the system to your students. In doing so, you will be better able to assess students regularly and keep track of those assessments. In the long run, you'll spend less time going over rules and routines and be able to focus more time on enhancing your students' writing.

Chapter 3

Looking Closely at the Units of Study With a Focus on Assessment

"Writing workshop turns the tables and puts kids in charge."

JoAnn Portalupi and Ralph Fletcher, (2001)
Writing Workshop: The Essential Guide

Throughout the school year you will expose your writers to various genres. With each genre come distinct goals to master. Your conference note sheets will cater to the characteristics of each genre (or other unit focus) as well as to the needs of each individual learner.

In this chapter you will find answers to the following questions:

- What are some possible writing units I might teach this year?
- What are my goals for each unit?
- Are there good mentor texts I can use to help me teach?
- How can I celebrate my students' work each month?
- How can I support the English language learners in my classroom?
- What might my students' work look like for each unit of study?
- How should my conference notes look?

Writing Units K–2 Overview

Kindergarten through second grade, students generally write in the same genres, and these genres become the topics of many of our units of study. However, we differentiate the goals of each unit to meet the needs of the writers in a particular grade. On the conference note sheets we've included in this chapter, the unit objectives at the top of each sheet are listed in a continuum of developing skills.

This continuum goes from the least complex skills to the most difficult skills. Therefore, as children progress through the primary grades, they should be able to achieve all the skills on the conference note sheets. Kindergarten children may only meet the most basic skills listed under the unit objectives. First graders should be able to achieve those basic skills as well as the more challenging skills described in the unit objectives. Second graders are expected to master all the skills listed in the objectives.

Each child will demonstrate varying levels of ability. Referring to your conference note sheet for each unit tells you what types of skills children should be able to master. This will give you insight into how each student is progressing through writing workshop. For example, first graders who are only succeeding in skills A–C might need extra support, whereas first graders who master skills A–G might need a challenge. The unit objectives will translate into mini-lessons that you teach as well as conference teaching points and small-group lessons. These objectives will guide your instruction during the unit, allowing each child to acquire new skills in his or her own time. This is why flexible assessment forms like the leveled writing conference notes we've designed are so helpful.

Nicole's | Classroom Notes

It's a big help to enlist parent support from the very beginning of the school year. During "Meet the Teacher" time, I always have a sign-up sheet listing different jobs that parents might like to do to help out the class. One of the biggest helps is the Celebration Coordinator. Before a celebration I usually enlist the help of two parents to help organize any food or decorations we might need. Sometimes the celebrations have themes centered around food, such as "international day" or "healthy eating." Having a parent coordinator helps me make sure that there are enough food and drinks for all our authors and guests, and it limits the work I have to put into the celebrations.

As a culmination of every writer's work and eventual mastery of skills, each unit ends in a celebration—and each unit should be celebrated in a different way. Children become excited about the celebrations and take pride in their work. They know they are writing for an audience and that the audience may change as the units change. Units generally last about one month. It's good practice to plan ahead of time for when your celebrations will take place. These "deadlines" make children feel like real authors and set a precedent for completing work in a timely manner. You may wish to note the celebrations at the start of the month on your class calendar. If you plan to invite parents or other guests, be sure to provide celebration dates in your school calendar or class newsletter.

Launching the Writing Workshop

As you launch the writing workshop at the beginning of the school year, children are learning the workshop rules and routines, the steps of the writing process, and how to tell a story. You may want to focus your mini-lessons on some of the skills outlined on the conference note sheet on page 43, or you may want to work on all of them. As always, consider the needs of the children in your class when deciding on your mini-lessons.

For each unit of study you should have a couple of mentor texts that you carry around to use during conferences. These

Objectives for Launching Writing Workshop unit
Print From CD/Copy From Appendix, page 107

texts are valuable tools for highlighting techniques that you want students to try. It's important to choose texts that match the focus genre for the unit. For the first month, it's helpful to plan ahead and read aloud books you're going to use in the upcoming units of study as mentor texts. *The Daddy Mountain* by Jules Feiffer (2004) is a simple, personal narrative that's great to start off the year with. Reading aloud *What Do Authors Do?* by Eileen Christelow (1995) will get students ready to become authors, too. Children will get a feel for what it's like to actually publish a book!

As the sample below shows, this kindergarten writer begins the year with a lot of knowledge about storytelling. Eesha includes characters and a setting in this story about a day with her friends. Compliments should focus on Eesha's mastery of unit objectives and might include her use of labels (F) and her ability to come up with story ideas (B). There are also several objectives that Eesha could work on, including choosing paper that is appropriate for her story (G) and adding more setting details to the illustration (J). The following sample shows what a conference note for Eesha's story might look like.

Eesha, a kindergartner, shows mastery of several skills in her story.

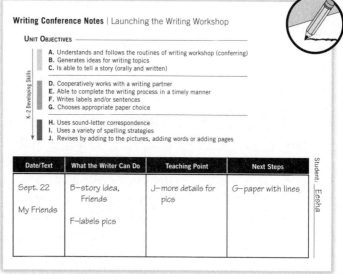

Writing Conference Notes | Launching the Writing Workshop

UNIT OBJECTIVES

A. Understands and follows the routines of writing workshop (conferring)
B. Generates ideas for writing topics
C. Is able to tell a story (orally and written)

D. Cooperatively works with a writing partner
E. Able to complete the writing process in a timely manner
F. Writes labels and/or sentences
G. Chooses appropriate paper choice

H. Uses sound-letter correspondence
I. Uses a variety of spelling strategies
J. Revises by adding to the pictures, adding words or adding pages

K–2 Developing Skills

Date/Text	What the Writer Can Do	Teaching Point	Next Steps
Sept. 22 My Friends	B—story idea, Friends F—labels pics	J—more details for pics	G—paper with lines

Student: Eesha

The teacher will work with Eesha on adding more details to her picture.

Explanation of Different Paper Choices and Purposes

Each child needs specific support structures to develop skills in writing. By providing different paper choices, you are nurturing and honing those skills. Paper Choice 1 allows your early writers to envision and create writing pieces that allow for illustrations with minimal text. Many of these early writers begin to use the space by constructing illustrations in the box and writing messages that involve forming letters or numbers on the line at the bottom of the page. They usually begin with random strings of letters.

In the next stage, writers may begin to write with greater detail and may need more lines to do so. Paper Choices 2 and 3 allow for more expression. These sheets may be stapled to become booklets that allow advanced kindergarteners to write across pages on a connected writing idea.

Paper Choices #1, #2, #3
Print From CD/Copy From
Appendix, pages 137–139

The two-page story on page 45 is the work of Steven, a first grader. By the second week of school, Steven already can stretch out a story across pages. He is able to tell a story through his writing (C), choose appropriate paper for his piece (G), and use letter-sound correspondence (H). Steven could work on adding setting to his pictures to create clarity for the reader (J) or using a writing partner to help ask him questions so that he may stretch his story even further (D). A sample conference note for his story appears below his work.

Within the first unit, it's beneficial to have two celebrations. When you begin the writing year with lots of routines and expectations of writing workshop, the writers in your classroom may lose sight of the purpose of writing. Two celebrations will help keep the momentum going in your classroom.

Many teachers choose to incorporate storytelling into the first unit. This helps children practice telling their story orally before writing it on paper. It also builds partnership skills and gets children accustomed to listening to each other. The first celebration could be a storyteller's celebration consisting of a simple round robin share with a small group of children. It's good practice to have four or five

First grader Steven has chosen the appropriate paper for his story.

children in each group. If parents are invited, make sure to assign at least one parent to each group to help monitor the celebration and ensure its success. A second celebration option at the end of the month is to have writing partners share one published piece with each other. It's best to start off the year with simple celebrations and create more elaborate ones as the students' writing develops.

Celebrations are meant to applaud all the writers in their best efforts to master the writing skills for the unit. Your individual conference note sheets will help you gauge how students have performed and how conferring in the next unit can proceed. You will be better able to monitor the students based on the notes you've taken and group them in the future for small-group instruction. These celebrations can also help build enthusiasm for the units to come.

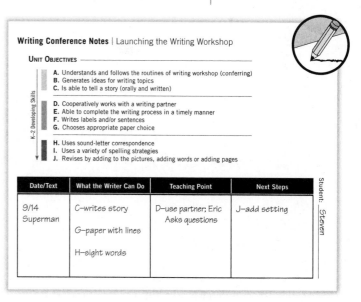

Writing Conference Notes | Launching the Writing Workshop

UNIT OBJECTIVES

K–2 Developing Skills

A. Understands and follows the routines of writing workshop (conferring)
B. Generates ideas for writing topics
C. Is able to tell a story (orally and written)

D. Cooperatively works with a writing partner
E. Able to complete the writing process in a timely manner
F. Writes labels and/or sentences
G. Chooses appropriate paper choice

H. Uses sound-letter correspondence
I. Uses a variety of spelling strategies
J. Revises by adding to the pictures, adding words or adding pages

Date/Text	What the Writer Can Do	Teaching Point	Next Steps
9/14 Superman	C–writes story G–paper with lines H–sight words	D–use partner; Eric Asks questions	J–add setting

Student: Steven

The teacher's next step will be to help Steven master the skill of adding setting details to his story.

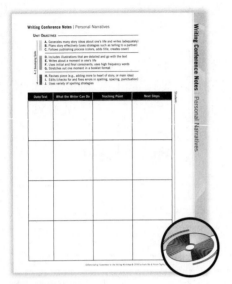

Objectives for Personal Narratives unit

Print From CD/Copy From Appendix, page 109

ELL Tip

Encourage English language learners to rely heavily on their illustrations by adding as many details as possible to tell the story. These children may feel most confident writing sight words and naming objects through labels. They can tell a story across pages through their pictures.

Personal Narratives

Personal narratives are small moments from children's lives that they choose to write about. These moments can be as simple as getting a paper cut or stepping on gum. Some children choose bigger events, such as the death of their pet or their first rollercoaster ride. Their lives are full of events they enjoy sharing, and they should be able to write many stories during the course of this unit. Children will use the skills they learned in the previous unit, such as orally telling a story, before writing on paper. They may start out by writing on one page and advance to three- or five-page booklets. As they continue developing their skills, writers begin to zoom in on their narrative moment by narrowing its focus and revising their piece. Children also learn and apply various grade-appropriate spelling strategies.

Many books written for the primary grades fit into the genre of personal narrative. Children at this age feel like they are a part of these stories and can often relate to the problems characters face. Some great mentor texts include *Knuffle Bunny* by Mo Willems (2004), *Come On, Rain!* by Karen Hesse (1999), *A Chair for My Mother* by Vera B. Williams (1982), and *Owl Moon* by Jane Yolen (1987). You might also look in your leveled library for simple texts to show students. These are wonderful conference tools since students can easily read them, and the text is appropriate for their capabilities.

In the example on page 47, second grader Georgia has stuck with one moment in her personal narrative (E). She also spells high-frequency words accurately (F). Teaching points may include using a booklet to stretch the story out (G) and adding more to the main idea (H).

Dunya, a kindergartner whose narrative appears on page 48, has drawn a detailed picture that matches the words on the page (D), can write high-frequency words (F), and even edits by including punctuation and appropriate spacing between words (I). She also has attempted to spell *park* with initial and final consonants—"pc." Dunya might improve her piece by adding a page (G) or publishing the piece by completing her coloring and adding a cover (C).

Personal narratives provide a good opportunity for parents to join in the publishing celebration. Students can leave their writing on their desks and walk around the room to read one

The Outside Read

Madison   Georgia

Read
Books

Book Fair

Read
Read
Everyday

Play T

People
Playing
Jumprope

by Georgia

The Outside
Read

Me and Madison were reading outside
she was reading in her mind. I also
was reading out loud. I was reading
before I could not say a word so I
ask Madison to help me. She help
and help when I could the word that
I can't say! Then play time was done. And
then all 2th grade went to eat lunch.

This second-grade student writes about reading outside with her friend.

another's work. Family members can read along with them. This type of celebration is like a "museum" exhibition. Children and adults may make compliments and comments about the work they read, and each student's writing piece is accompanied by a comment sheet (see Celebration Comment Sheet, page 30). Another option is to allow children to read their piece in front of the class and guests. If you have a microphone available, this will help to amplify soft voices. Since student work tends to be short at the start of the school year, it won't take too long for everyone to read their writing pieces.

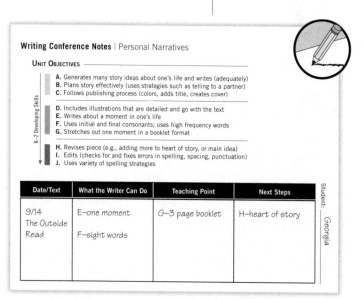

Writing Conference Notes | Personal Narratives

UNIT OBJECTIVES

K–2 Developing Skills

A. Generates many story ideas about one's life and writes (adequately)
B. Plans story effectively (uses strategies such as telling to a partner)
C. Follows publishing process (colors, adds title, creates cover)

D. Includes illustrations that are detailed and go with the text
E. Writes about a moment in one's life
F. Uses initial and final consonants; uses high frequency words
G. Stretches out one moment in a booklet format

H. Revises piece (e.g., adding more to heart of story, or main idea)
I. Edits (checks for and fixes errors in spelling, spacing, punctuation)
J. Uses variety of spelling strategies

Date/Text	What the Writer Can Do	Teaching Point	Next Steps
9/14 The Outside Read	E—one moment F—sight words	G—3 page booklet	H—heart of story

Student: Georgia

The teacher will focus on helping Georgia expand her personal narrative to three pages.

I am in the park.

This kindergarten student accompanies her personal narrative drawing with text.

Unit Objectives

A. Generates many story ideas about one's life and writes (adequately)
B. Plans story effectively (uses strategies such as telling to a partner)
C. Follows publishing process (colors, adds title, creates cover)

D. Includes illustrations that are detailed and go with the text
E. Writes about a moment in one's life
F. Uses initial and final consonants; uses high frequency words
G. Stretches out one moment in a booklet format

H. Revises piece (e.g., adding more to heart of story, or main idea)
I. Edits (checks for and fixes errors in spelling, spacing, punctuation)
J. Uses variety of spelling strategies

K–2 Developing Skills

Date/Text	What the Writer Can Do	Teaching Point	Next Steps
10/9 The Park	D–pics match words	C–publish	G–add pages
	F–pc for park		
	I–period/spaces		

Student: Dunya

The conference note sheet shows that Dunya has mastered skills D, F, and I.

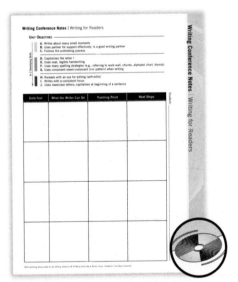

Objectives for Writing for Readers unit
Print From CD/Copy From Appendix, page 110

Writing for Readers

Students usually benefit from writing personal narratives throughout the school year, beginning with a focus on the content of the writing. Once they have mastered the appropriate skills from the first two sections of the personal narrative objective list (see above), it's time to shift the focus to conventions. Students will work on spelling, capitalization, punctuation, and penmanship. The goal is for student writing to be readable by an audience.

It's useful to photocopy student work to use as mentor texts for this unit. Choose work that highlights the conventions you want students to work on. You can also create errors in your personal writing samples to teach conventions. Laminate these pieces and carry them around for conferences. When you introduce your teaching point, you can model how to edit the pieces using an overhead marker. In this way, you can later erase your corrections and use the pieces over and over again.

Keeping this goal in mind, a good celebration for this unit is to have students choose a piece to give as a gift to someone special. Give each student a manila folder to decorate as the wrapping paper. They may choose to give their piece to a family member, a friend, a teacher, or a classmate, or if you wish, all children may give their piece to a classmate or their writing buddy from another class. Everyone can open their gift at the same time and try to read the pieces. Students can also use "editing glasses" to help read student work more clearly. Editing work will become more evident when they can "see" with their editing glasses. During the celebration, editors can read student work with a fresh view. The more readable the work, the more successful that student was in the unit.

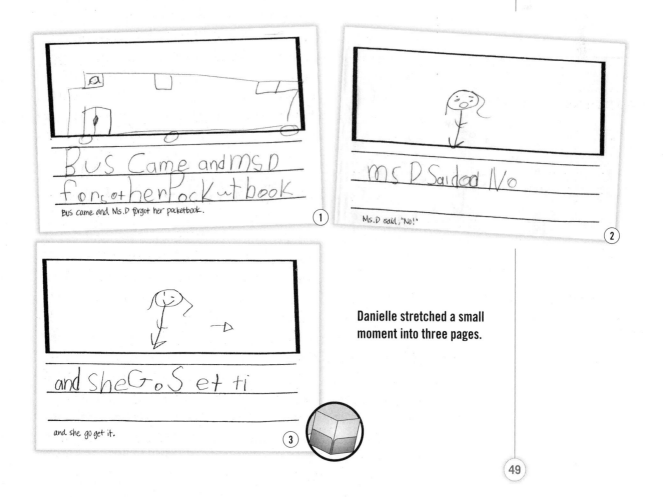

Bus came and Ms. D forgot her pocketbook. ①

Ms. D said, "No!" ②

and she go get it. ③

Danielle stretched a small moment into three pages.

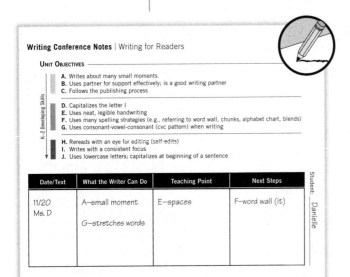

Writing Conference Notes | Writing for Readers

UNIT OBJECTIVES

A. Writes about many small moments
B. Uses partner for support effectively; is a good writing partner
C. Follows the publishing process

D. Capitalizes the letter I
E. Uses neat, legible handwriting
F. Uses many spelling strategies (e.g., referring to word wall, chunks, alphabet chart, blends)
G. Uses consonant-vowel-consonant (cvc pattern) when writing

H. Rereads with an eye for editing (self-edits)
I. Writes with a consistent focus
J. Uses lowercase letters; capitalizes at beginning of a sentence

Date/Text	What the Writer Can Do	Teaching Point	Next Steps
11/20 Ms. D	A—small moment G—stretches words	E—spaces	F—word wall (it)

Student: Danielle

The teacher will focus on helping Danielle add spaces between words.

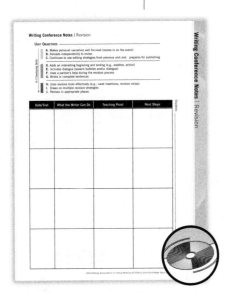

Writing Conference Notes | Revision

UNIT OBJECTIVES

A. Makes personal narrative well focused (zooms in on the event)
B. Rereads independently to revise
C. Continues to use editing strategies from previous unit and prepares for publishing

D. Adds an interesting beginning and ending (e.g., weather, action)
E. Includes dialogue (speech bubbles and/or dialogue)
F. Uses a partner's help during the revision process
G. Writes in complete sentences

H. Uses revision tools effectively (e.g., carat insertions, revision strips)
I. Draws on multiple revision strategies
J. Revises in appropriate places

Date/Text	What the Writer Can Do	Teaching Point	Next Steps

Objectives for Revision unit
Print From CD/Copy From Appendix, page 111

In the story on the previous page, kindergartener Danielle writes about her teacher forgetting her purse (A) and attempts to stretch out words by adding many letters to match the sounds she hears (G). She could work on her handwriting by adding better spacing between words and not erasing (E). She might also try using the word wall to write sight words like *it* and *get* (F). The sample at left shows how a conference note might look.

Revision

Although you have introduced students to some basic revision skills such as "adding on," this unit gives them an opportunity to focus more deeply on the revision aspect of the writing process. This in-depth study reviews the strategies they know while introducing new revision strategies. Writers also become familiar with revision tools. You may choose to give out colored revision pens or pencils. This makes it easy to see where students are revising. Some students may be successful at using revision strips: They write their latest additions on strips of paper and cut and tape or glue the writing where it belongs. Other children may use more standard methods to add on, such as like asterisks (*) and carets (^). Students can revise new pieces that they are creating on the spot or look back at old work (even published pieces) and revise those.

It's a good idea to revisit your personal narrative read-alouds during this unit of study. Since children have heard these books many times and are familiar with their plots, they can focus in on special crafts the authors used as revision strategies. For example, in *Knuffle Bunny* (2004), Mo Willems effectively uses transitional language and dialogue in the form of speech bubbles. Jane Yolen in *Owl Moon* (1987) uses a lot of beautiful, descriptive language to help us picture the setting. She also starts by describing the setting, which children can try out in their own pieces.

You may also want to introduce a new personal narrative to showcase additional techniques published authors use. A good choice would be *Whistling* by Elizabeth Partridge (2003). Children can easily relate to the idea of learning how to whistle.

Partridge's use of action words, dialogue, and onomatopoeia are techniques to point out to students. When teaching the craft of show, not tell, in which authors show feelings through what the characters say and do rather than telling the feeling words, the book *I Love My Hair* by Natasha Anastasia Tarpley (1998) is a great mentor text. Remember to have a few texts nearby when conferring with students.

Many teachers may wish to start off by having students brainstorm some possible story ideas. This helps children get started right away when it's time to draft. In the sample below, first grader Raymond has done a great job of picking out focused moments (A). Because his ideas are focused, this would be an excellent time to discuss how to introduce a piece. His teacher might have him orally tell the story and create several possible beginnings to choose from (D). If Raymond's beginning sounded good, the next step might be to encourage the inclusion of dialogue in the piece (E).

Children tend to get very excited about the revision unit, especially when they are given special revision "tools" like colored pens.

ELL Tip

Many English language learners will accidentally leave out words in their writing. Teach these students how to use a caret (^) to insert words. A writing partner might help her ELL peer find places where adding a word will help the piece make sense. You may also wish to pull small groups of English language learners together to explicitly address common usage issues such as how to use the appropriate gender-specific pronouns and verb tense. ELLs who are in the acquisition phase may focus on adding to the pictures as a great revision tool.

Raymond focuses on the topic of kid problems to generate story ideas.

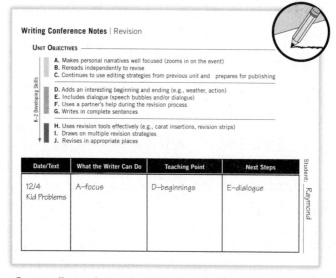

Raymond's teacher praised him for focusing well on story ideas.

Yuria, a second grader, even chose to write a story about revision pens!

Writing Conference Notes | Revision

UNIT OBJECTIVES

K–2 Developing Skills

A. Makes personal narratives well focused (zooms in on the event)
B. Rereads independently to revise
C. Continues to use editing strategies from previous unit and prepares for publishing

D. Adds an interesting beginning and ending (e.g., weather, action)
E. Includes dialogue (speech bubbles and/or dialogue)
F. Uses a partner's help during the revision process
G. Writes in complete sentences

H. Uses revision tools effectively (e.g., carat insertions, revision strips)
I. Draws on multiple revision strategies
J. Revises in appropriate places

Date/Text	What the Writer Can Do	Teaching Point	Next Steps
12/13 Yeah revision pens!	I—thoughts/tension G—complete sent. E—dialogue	I—more action	J—good spots

Student: Yuria

The teacher will guide Yuria in revising her story to show more action.

In the sample shown here, Yuria includes a lot of her internal thinking and builds tension throughout the story (I), which is an advanced revision strategy. She writes in complete sentences, which makes the piece readable (G). Although Yuria has a lot of dialogue (E), she could work on adding more action to the piece (I) and think about good places to put in action and setting details (J).

Some students, like Jessica whose work appears on page 53, choose to go back to their old personal narratives and revise them to make them better. This first grader has chosen a piece from the previous month and used revision pencils well (H). Her writing partner helped her find the heart of the story (marked off with a heart-shaped sticky note) and add more to that part (A, D, E, F, G, H, I, J). Jessica's piece reflects all the revision strategies that she has learned—in fact, she even chose ones that weren't taught. In a case like this, when all the unit objectives have been circled or checked off, you might take the opportunity to simply encourage the student to reread the piece and realize no more revision is necessary (B). It's time to work on revising a different writing piece. Jessica's teacher may also wish to work on editing with her in the future (C).

As a culminating activity, you can create a revision museum—a display of students' writing that highlights the revision skills they've learned to use—and invite parents to celebrate the published writing of the revision unit. (You may want to use the invitation form shown on page 53 as a template.)

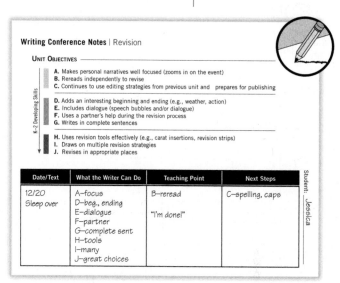

The teacher plans to focus on spelling and capitalization as Jessica later edits her piece.

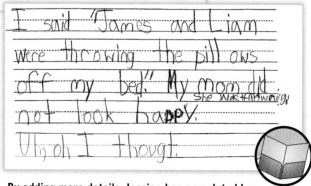

By adding more details, Jessica has completed her revision successfully.

To create the museum pieces, writers can pick three revision strategies they tried out and post them on sticky notes throughout their writing piece. The sticky notes might say, "Check out how I tried a new beginning here!" or "Look at how I took out a part that didn't fit!" Other children might use heart-shaped sticky notes to mark the heart of their story—the place that is most important. In this spot, writers note the different revision strategies they used to enhance their piece. In this way, readers can quickly and easily locate revision strategies used on the page, and they are able to be more specific in their comments, compliments, or questions.

Invitation
Print From CD/Copy
From Appendix, page 135

Objectives for Author's Craft Study unit
Print From CD/Copy From Appendix, page 112

Author's Craft Study

In a craft study, students learn from an author that the class has chosen to study. It's important to choose someone whose writing is the kind your students are capable of emulating. Look at the size of the books, the use of pictures to support words, and sentence structure.

Donald Crews and Angela Johnson are good mentor authors for kindergarteners; Ezra Jack Keats and Frank Asch are good choices for first grade. Second graders who need a bit of a challenge might find success with Judith Viorst or Cynthia Rylant. Students will begin to read these books with an eye for authors' craft. Once they are able to name what the author is doing, they can try it out in their own writing. Some techniques to look out for are ellipses for suspense, repetition for emphasis, and listing to give examples, as well as anything else you want students to do in their writing. They can even learn how to illustrate like the author they are studying. For example, Frank Asch usually creates a dedication page with many scenes. Students can try this technique in their own work. When it's editing time, they may notice the conventions of print their author uses, like capitalizing names or using bold print, and try to edit like the author they are studying. In emulating the techniques of real authors, students feel like real authors too.

Charles, a first grader, is studying Frank Asch. In his story, shown on page 55, Charles remembers to write a "zoomed-in" personal narrative that he has learned from past units (A). His topic of looking for his mom is simple yet interesting. Like Asch, Charles uses the listing technique by naming all of the places he looked for his mom before finding her in the basement doing the laundry. He also uses dialogue, speech bubbles, ellipses, and begins his story with the weather, just as Asch does (I, J). Charles might now use an editing checklist to prepare for publishing (G).

As you complete the unit, many of your writers will have tried out many crafting techniques. A published piece by Yancy, a first grader (page 56), highlights many techniques used by his mentor, Ezra Jack Keats. In his piece, Yancy includes internal dialogue, repeated words, interesting word choices ("running like the speed of light"), boldface words, and ellipses to build suspense (I). He also remembers to use revision strategies taught in the previous unit, adding revision strips to lengthen his piece and using asterisks to guide his readers along the way (D). He concludes his piece with a dedication page and an about-the-author page (F).

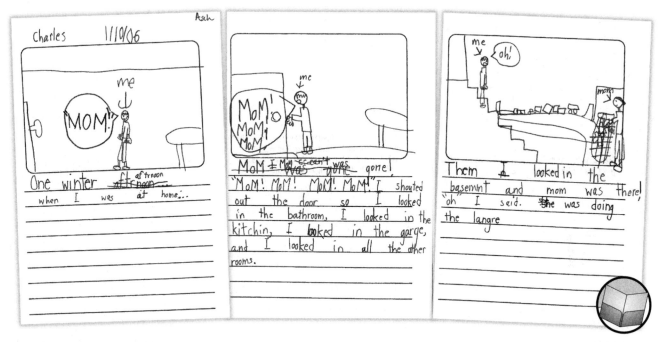

Charles emulates author Frank Asch in his small-moment narrative.

A great celebration for the Author's Craft Study unit is to have an Author Appreciation Day. Children can write letters to the authors they've studied all month long and thank them for the crafts they've come to love and rely on in their own writing. In the letters, students show and name the crafts they've learned.

Your conference note sheets will help you to assess the specific skills the writers in your class have demonstrated and named in their writing pieces. These notes will allow you to document how your students have integrated the authors' techniques and the level of sophistication with which they've applied those skills in their own writing. Children can even send their letters to the author in hopes that the author will write back. This is a good time to do some research and find information to share with students about their authors.

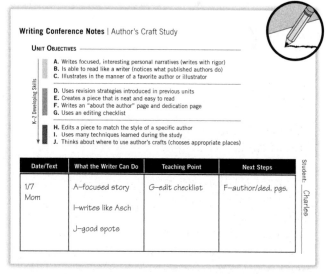

Later, Charles might create an about-the-author page and a dedication page for his piece, thereby addressing objective F.

Another celebration idea is to throw a fancy party. After reading *Fancy Nancy* by Jane O'Connor (2006) and learning how to be "fancy" all month long, children can come to school dressed up and ready to celebrate the new ways they've learned to write. Parents can decorate the classroom to set the tone of an elegant affair.

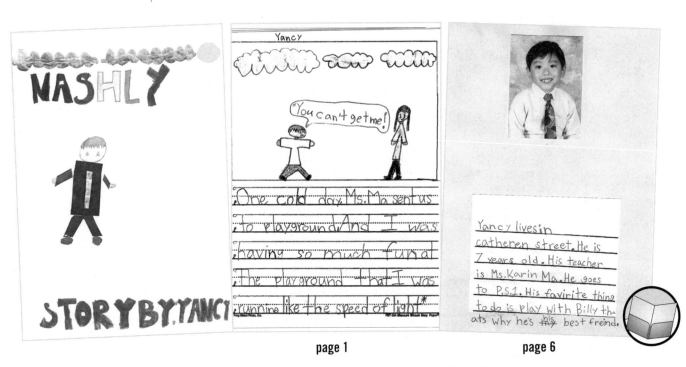

page 1   page 6

Yancy also learned that many books have an About the Author page
and attempted to create one of his own in his book *Nashly*.

Nicole's | Classroom Notes

After our study of Judith Viorst, my classroom was transformed into an elegant affair. For our fancy party, students tried using fancy things like big words. Children and parents had so much fun dressing up for the celebration. We planned it to occur right after lunch so that parents could set up the room while the class was away and surprise students when they returned. The looks on their faces were priceless. It was helpful to have extra hats, party favors, boas, ties, and tiaras for guests who forgot to get fancy. Children really emphasized good word choice in their writing pieces as well as their future stories, and their vocabulary improved a lot that year.

After studying Judith Viorst's writing all month, Bailey,
a second grader, wrote her a letter of appreciation.

Nonfiction: How-To's

How-to writing can be done throughout the primary grades to introduce young writers to nonnarrative writing or to reinforce key nonfiction skills and concepts. When the genre is first introduced in kindergarten, it may take more time to complete this unit of study. However, as students become more accustomed to writing how-to's, the unit can be shortened. In second grade, you may choose to have students complete a how-to within your All About unit of study. For example, if a writer chooses the topic of dogs, a possible how-to angle could be How to Train Your Dog.

When helping kindergarteners find topics, teachers would do well to consider classroom tasks that their students are capable of doing. These can become topics for the whole class to work on together during shared writing. Unpacking, washing your hands, fire drills, and tying your shoelaces make good topics. This unit also helps children develop better listening skills as they learn how to complete certain daily tasks.

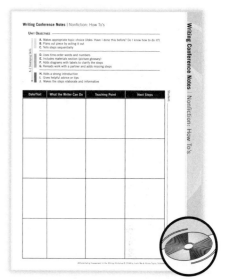

Objectives for Nonfiction: How-To's unit
Print From CD/Copy From Appendix, page 113

Our | Classroom Notes

At the start of the school year, we create charts that teach children how to follow basic classroom routines. Students are not aware of it, but these charts are actually how-to's. In this way, by the time students learn about how-to's, they've already been exposed to the genre. We refer to the charts we created earlier in the school year, and students feel more confident that they can try this format during writing time.

The writer's goal during this unit is to teach someone else how to do something that he or she may not be familiar with. You can help students generate topic ideas by pointing out how-to's in their everyday lives, including simple recipes they may know (s'mores, peanut-butter-and-jelly sandwiches) or directions for classroom games (Chutes and Ladders, Connect Four). Having students participate in following directions shows them what how-to's are and helps them figure out what good topics may sound like. Directions can start out very simply with a one-sentence command for each step, accompanied by a simple illustration. As students progress through the grades, how-to's can get more elaborate with the addition of special features including diagrams, introductions, captions, and advice to readers.

Balcony Garden by Rebecca Weber (1998) and *Art Smart: How to Draw Dinosaurs* by Christine Smith (1996) make excellent mentor texts for this unit. Remember to represent a diversity of topics so that children can see many possibilities for the how-to's they will create.

In the sample below, Sumia found a topic she knew about—getting dressed (A). and included a picture glossary to illustrate everything a girl needs to get dressed (E). It would be a good idea to encourage her to plan out the steps by acting it out (B). Later, when Sumia writes the how-to, the teacher might make sure she includes sequential words and numbers (D).

At the end of the year, students may choose to reflect on all the genres they've learned throughout writing workshop, and pick a genre they liked to write in. As students begin to choose specific genres to write in, you can go back to that unit's class checklist sheet. If you notice that the writer has continued to demonstrate skills specific to that unit in her new writing, then she has truly mastered those skills. Additionally, this process gives you another opportunity to revisit skills that students may not have mastered.

Kindergarteners require a clear format to guide them.

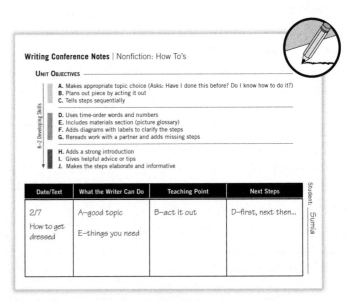

As a next step, the teacher could also work with Sumia on objective F, labeling all illustrations.

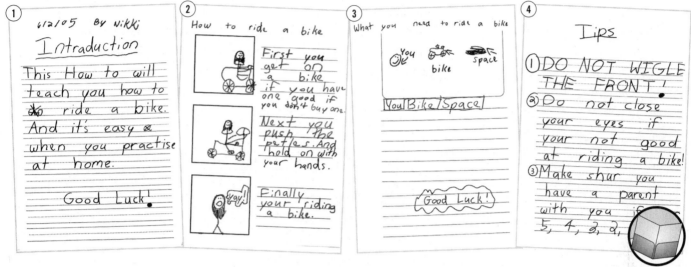

Nicolette, a first grader, remembered the how-to unit of study.

In the sample above, Nicolette chose to teach others how to ride a bike. Independently, she recalls the sequential steps and uses sequential words such as *first*, *next*, and *finally* (C, D). After meeting with her teacher, Nicolette thinks about her teacher's advice and considers what other elements how-to's might have. She adds an introduction, a picture glossary, and tips (H, I, E). Clearly, Nicolette still meets the how-to unit objectives several months after the unit was completed. The teacher feels confident that Nicolette knows what a how-to is all about and can refer back to the class checklist and mark this.

A great celebration for a how-to unit is to create a class sign-up sheet. The class generates a list of their how-to topics, and children sign up to read and learn more about the topic that interests them most. Writers learn the power of instructional writing through this celebration. They are aware that their writing is purposeful and written for an audience. If the readers are able to successfully follow the steps and end up with the desired outcome, then writers have succeeded in achieving the skills outlined in the assessment notes.

Other great celebrations include using a special recipe or art project and attempting to successfully follow directions while having fun. You may also encourage each student to write a recipe as a how-to. Students could then have a cooking show where they bring in the ingredients and tools and showcase their recipes.

Want To Learn Something New?		
How to...	Presented by...	Sign Up
grow a flower	Jenny	Nancy
Make a paper plane	Paul	Tony
kick the soccer ball	Baiely	Emira
Feed your dog	Samantha	Derek
make popcorn	Tony	Roy

Emira has signed up to read Baiely's how-to on kicking a soccer ball.

Everyone gets to taste some of the special treats. Simple recipes include trail mix and "worms in dirt" (chocolate pudding with gummy worms). Remind children that these recipes should not require the use of an oven.

Nonfiction: All About Books

After working on narrative pieces for many months, writers often discover a new enthusiasm for writing nonfiction. This enthusiasm stems from students' exposure to reading nonfiction texts by authors such as Gail Gibbons throughout the year before beginning this unit. A wonderful nonfiction author, Gibbons covers a variety of topics in her books, from plants to animals to jobs. Two books we like to use are *The Seasons of Arnold's Apple Tree* (1984) and *The Post Office Book: Mail and How It Moves* (1982). There are also some good leveled books like *Black and White* by Dorothy Avery (1998). It's easy to find many nonfiction features in all these books to show students during conference time.

The goal of this unit is for the writer to teach people a lot of information about a topic. The information children will write is based on their prior knowledge of the topic, so most primary teachers choose to have students complete this unit without any research. Some basic research can be conducted if students are ready for a challenge. Have them read books about their topics, ask others about the topic, and find information on the Internet.

Picking topics that they know a lot about ensures that students are on the right track before they begin this unit, so you may wish to have them select several topics, and later make the final decision about which topic is best for them to pursue. By second grade, some writers are very familiar with this style of writing. They should be able to choose topics more independently and write more pieces. Therefore, it's possible for these students to create two published books including one in which they gather research about a topic that interests them, organize this information, and create a book to showcase what they've learned.

Providing scaffolded formats helps guide writers toward using special features that are found frequently in nonfiction books. Be aware, too, that choice of paper for nonfiction writing can vary in different grades. It helps to differentiate for the different grade levels. The greater variety of format choices you offer, the better students can fully demonstrate their knowledge of the genre.

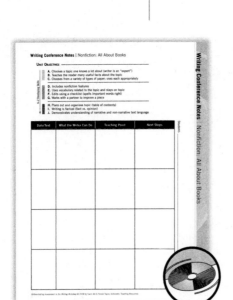

Objectives for Nonfiction: All About Books unit

Print From CD/Copy From Appendix, page 114

Karin's | Classroom Notes

When my students choose a nonfiction topic, I always pull books from the classroom library about their specific topics. I encourage children to read about their topic before writing workshop, usually during independent reading time. This way, they end up remembering a lot more information for their own books, which makes their work more factual. My students really end up teaching their readers a lot about their topic. Their vocabulary increases as well!

Print From CD/Copy From Appendix, pages 140–142

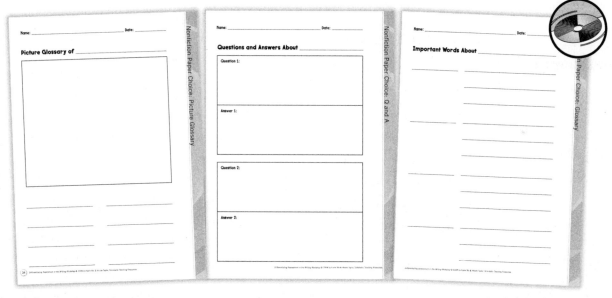

Students can list things that are related to their topic and draw illustrations to match on a picture glossary.

First graders are naturally inquisitive, which makes the question-and-answer format the perfect paper choice for them.

Students in second grade can identify important words related to their topic and identify them on the glossary page.

The paper choice serves as a visual reminder to help students know what to do and to get their ideas across more easily. Photographs can also be useful. Have students bring in different photographs to incorporate into their piece.

The objectives listed for this unit are general, but you may wish to be more specific in your note taking by listing the features the students choose to use. These features will show you where your students stand on the continuum of writing skills. For instance, children who are able to complete the Important Words About glossary page are writing at a more sophisticated level than those using the Picture Glossary page (both shown above).

ELL Tip

It's important to help English language learners build vocabulary. Writing about a familiar theme allows these children to get to know new vocabulary words. Paper choice also helps them. They will have many opportunities to label pictures. For example, a child writing about pigs will draw a pig and label the body parts. These writers begin to develop vocabulary and meaning by writing words that are connected.

Emily, a second grader, chose a topic she was an expert on: shopping (A). Her piece successfully teaches people a lot of information (B), uses a variety of scaffolded formats effectively (C), and contains nonfiction features including a table of contents, introduction, how-to, and diagram (D, H). Her piece could be enhanced with the use of photographs (F). To encourage her to say more, she might work with a partner who could ask her questions about shopping (G). The conference note sheet shown below comments on Emily's work:

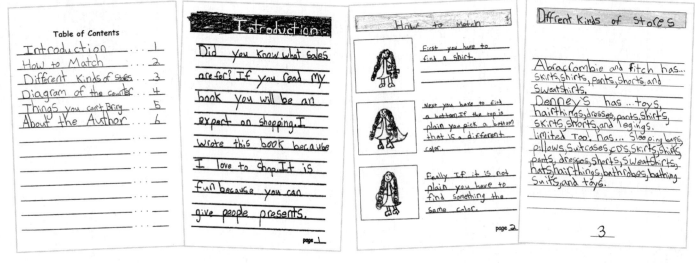

Table of Contents
Introduction 1
How to Match 2
Different Kinds of Stores . 3
Diagram of the counter . . 4
Things you can't Bring . . 5
About the Author . . . 6

Introduction

Did you Know what sales are for? If you read My book you will be an expart on shopping. I wrote this book because I love to shop. It is fun because you can give people presents.

page 1

How to Match

First you have to find a shirt.

Next you have to find a bottom. If the top is plain you pick a bottom that is a different color.

Finally If it is not plain you have to find Something the same color.

page 2

Diffrent Kinds of Stores

Abraccombie and fitch has... skirts, shirts, pants, shorts, and sweatshirts.
Denney's has... toys, hairthings, dresses, pants, shirts, skirts, shorts, and legings.
limited Too! has... Sleeping bags, pillows, Suitcases, CD's, skirts, shirts, pants, dresses, shorts, sweatshirts, hats, hairthings, bathrobes, bathing Suits, and toys.

3

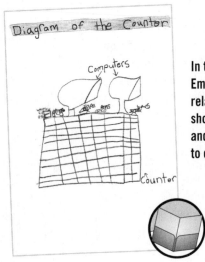

Diagram of the Counter

Computers

pens

Counter

In this piece on shopping, Emily uses vocabulary related to the topic of shopping, such as *match* and *counter*, which relate to objective E.

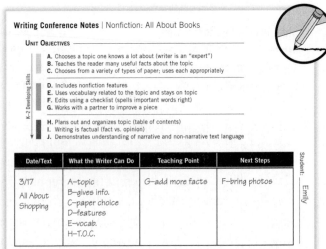

Writing Conference Notes | Nonfiction: All About Books

UNIT OBJECTIVES

A. Chooses a topic one knows a lot about (writer is an "expert")
B. Teaches the reader many useful facts about the topic
C. Chooses from a variety of types of paper; uses each appropriately

D. Includes nonfiction features
E. Uses vocabulary related to the topic and stays on topic
F. Edits using a checklist (spells important words right)
G. Works with a partner to improve a piece

H. Plans out and organizes topic (table of contents)
I. Writing is factual (fact vs. opinion)
J. Demonstrates understanding of narrative and non-narrative text language

K–2 Developing Skills

Date/Text	What the Writer Can Do	Teaching Point	Next Steps
3/17 All About Shopping	A—topic B—gives info. C—paper choice D—features E—vocab. H—T.O.C.	G—add more facts	F—bring photos

Student: Emily

Emily shows mastery in six of the objectives for a nonfiction how-to.

SIX LEGGED CREATURES
BY CLASS 1-5

PHOTOGRAPHS PROVIDED BY STEVEN

Table of Contents

	Page Number
What is an insect?	1
What do insects look like?	2
How do bees make honey? ...	5
Do butterflies change?	9

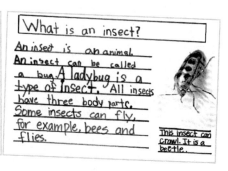

What is an insect?

An insect is an animal. An insect can be called a bug. A ladybug is a type of insect. All insects have three body parts. Some insects can fly, for example, bees and flies.

This insect can crawl. It is a beetle.

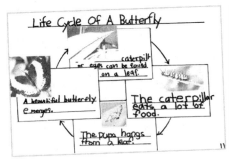

Life Cycle Of A Butterfly

caterpillar or eggs can be found on a leaf.

A beautiful butterfly emerges.

The caterpillar eats a lot of food.

The pupa hangs from a leaf.

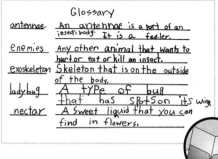

Glossary

antennae   An antennae is a part of an insect's body. It is a feeler.

enemies   Any other animal that wants to hurt or eat or kill an insect.

exoskeleton   Skeleton that is on the outside of the body.

ladybug   A type of bug that has spots on its wing

nectar   A sweet liquid that you can find in flowers.

First-grade students worked together to include all the nonfiction features their teacher introduced to them, such as a cover with photographs and photo credits.

A first-grade class compiled a class nonfiction book about six-legged creatures. Pages from their book are featured above. Most of the students were English language learners, who benefited from teacher support in creating this nonfiction text.

As your nonfiction writing unit comes to a close, you can use your conference note sheets and the class checklist sheet to help you to group the skill levels of the writers in your class. You can pair writers of similar abilities to share their pieces. Have students celebrate the features they used by putting sticky notes on the ones they wish to showcase in their book. Then they can meet with a partner to explain how those features help teach readers about the topic.

Another celebration possibility is to split the class into small groups and send them into other primary classrooms to share a section from their books. Look closely at student work and determine the level of work produced. Children whose pieces are extremely informative can go to the upper grades to share, while the simplest pieces can be shared with younger-grade students. In this way, all students feel successful and will receive appropriate feedback from their peers. You can also create a rubric or a checklist to allow peers to assess one another's work. Your rubric or checklist can include the skills you've taught for the unit, enabling students to evaluate with a keen eye and give advice to their fellow writers.

When I send children to classes around the school, I make sure I ask my colleagues' permission far in advance. I pick the end of the school day to do this so we will not interrupt student learning. My students get a lot of positive feedback from their intervisitations. Advanced writers feel great pride when they receive praise from older children. One student even received a set of letters from the fifth-grade class thanking her for her visit—she beamed with joy—and the fifth graders learned some new information from her nonfiction piece.

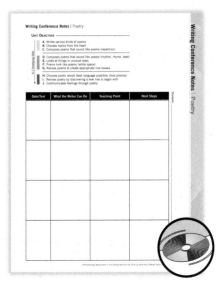

Objectives for the Poetry unit
Print From CD/Copy From Appendix, page 115

Poetry

Poetry is a fun unit in which all children can feel successful. As the unit progresses, their confidence grows, and soon they may attempt several poems in one writing period. Read various styles and forms of poetry to children so they can emulate different poets in their writing. The more that children read poetry and listen to it being read aloud, the easier it is for them to transfer repetition, rhythm, powerful language, white space, and line breaks to their own writing.

Some excellent poetry anthologies that young children enjoy include *Splish Splash* (1994) by Joan Bransfield Graham and *Fathers, Mothers, Sisters, Brothers: A Collection of Family Poems* by Mary Ann Hoberman (1991). Since children will most likely end the unit by creating their own poetry anthology, it's important to show them what an anthology looks like and how it might be organized. Hoberman chose to collect poems around the theme of family. Graham picked poems that related to a theme, but she reformatted the poems into playful shapes. All the poems in her anthology are shape poems. Since there will be an emphasis on developing poetic language during this unit, Jonathan London's *When the Fireflies Came* (1985) is also a wonderful mentor text to use.

In the poem on page 65 (top right), Jennifer, a kindergarten student, chose a topic that meant a lot to her (B). She used repetition to get her point across to the audience (C). Her poem also looked like a poem (F, G). Her poem truly gets across her feelings about God (J).

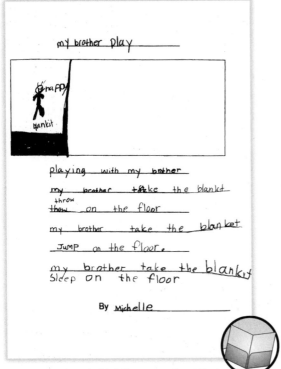

my brother play

playing with my brother
my brother take the blankit
throw them on the floor
my brother take the blanket
jump on the floor.
my brother take the blankit
sleep on the floor

By Michelle

Listing poems, which list several words connected to a theme or topic, are often simple starting points for young poets.

God

I love God
God is in my
heart
He let's us
have names
He let's us
have poems
He let's us
have stars.

By Jennifer

Jennifer chose a format in which the lines are almost all the same length.

Again, the unit objectives help you to reach the goals based on each student's needs. As you reflect and review your notes, you may start to plan for a celebration when you notice that many of your writers have mastered the skills listed in the objectives.

A marvelous celebration for this unit is to take the class on a poetry parade around the school or the neighborhood. Children can create signs and sing the chant below as they hand out copies of their poems to the community.

ELL Tip

English language learners, who are often hesitant during writing time, tend to shine during this unit of study, which frees them from the pressures of proper grammar and punctuation and allows them to play with words.

Poet's Cheer
ABCDEFG
Poetry is for you and me!
HIJKLMN
We hope that we can do it again.
OPQRSTU
We wrote more than just a few.
VWXY and Z
Amazing poet, that is me!
Sound off 1, 2.
Sound off 3, 4.
1, 2, 3, 4!

We created the "Poet's Cheer" as a part of our poetry parade around the neighborhood. A nearby shopping center with many stores and restaurants was easy to visit. We made copies of published poems and took a neighborhood walk. Parents came along for the fun as we passed out copies of our work to enthusiastic passersby. Many of the children's poems were posted on store windows.

Another idea for a celebration is a poet's café, in which children have milk and cookies as other writers recite their poetry in the style of an open-mic night. A microphone is useful here, especially if parents are invited. Guests get to enjoy hearing writing about objects, themes, and feelings in a new way. The young poets always recite their poems with great expression and passion.

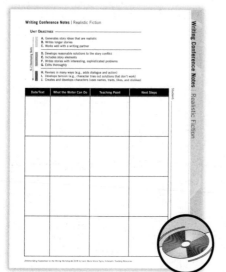

Objectives for Realistic Fiction unit
Print From CD/Copy From Appendix,
page 116

Realistic Fiction

"If your characters are going to come alive on the page, they must first come alive in your mind. This may seem strange, but that's the way a writer's imagination works. You've got to start envisioning them—faces, quirks, fears—in order for them to become real."

RALPH FLETCHER, (1999) *LIVE WRITING: BREATHING LIFE INTO YOUR WORDS*

Realistic fiction writing allows children to use their imagination and knowledge of storytelling. Students can base their story ideas on their life experiences and stretch the truth by inventing characters, changing the setting, or altering the sequence of events. As students become more proficient writers, their characters come to life, tension mounts, and various crafts are present. It's ideal to do this unit in the spring so that students may incorporate all the authors' crafts they've learned in the previous writing units.

Some realistic fiction picture books that children really enjoy are *Ruby and Bubbles* by Rosie Winstead (2006), *Odd Velvet* by Mary E. Whitcomb (1998), *"Let's Get a Pup!" Said Kate* by Bob Graham (2001), *Wilson Sat Alone* by Debra Hess (1994), and *No Haircut Today!* by Elivia Savadier (2005). The problems these characters face are kid-friendly, and the plots are interesting to read. Many series that children read throughout the school year fall into the genre of realistic fiction. *Henry and Mudge* by Cynthia Rylant (1987), *Pinky and Rex* by James Howe (1990), and *Biscuit* by Alyssa Satin Capucilli (1996) are all excellent mentor texts. Using a series of books as mentor texts encourages children to write multiple realistic fiction books based on the same character, and some students even attempt to write chapter books.

Writing workshop often leads to many story ideas for students. First grader Tiffany had a writing block until she developed the realistic fiction story shown below around a real event in her own life. Since the event happened to her, she knows her problem and solution are believable (A, D, F). Tiffany edits very thoroughly, which is evident by her crossing out words and trying to spell them accurately (G). Her lengthy story (B) includes story elements (E) and shows the use of several revision strategies taught previously (H). Assessing Tiffany's work, it's clear she has accomplished the basic and challenging objectives, which leaves the teacher to work on the hardest skills. This will help Tiffany's writing reach its full potential. In the future, she can work on developing tension (I).

The writer of "Blue Ink," the sample piece on page 68, demonstrates mastery in almost every objective except the final one. She could more fully develop her character, Lemon (J). The teacher may also choose to work on revision by having the writer take away parts that may be unnecessary (H).

The writer of "Blue Ink," the sample piece on page 68

ELL Tip

Reading aloud familiar books from previous units gives English language learners an understanding of how these stories should sound. It also helps them get ideas for problems to include in their stories. *The Snowy Day* (1962) and *Whistle for Willie* (1977) by Ezra Jack Keats are great choices for reading aloud. Another idea is to use simple guided reading books as read-alouds for a small group of ELLs. Some possibilities include *Poochie the Poodle* by Danielle Gamble (2004) and *The Whistle Tooth* by Alan Trussell-Cullen (1998). These texts are closer to the writing primary students are capable of doing. The simple plots demonstrate how students' stories should develop.

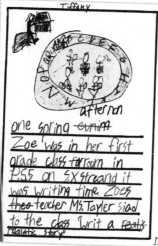
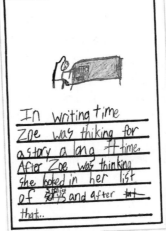
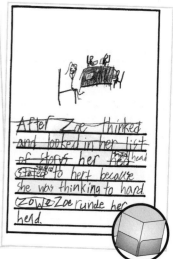

Tiffany turned a small moment in her own life into realistic fiction (cover, and pages 1–3 shown).

Students will be ready to publish when they incorporate the skills of this unit into their narrative pieces. As before, you'll note each writer's attempts to master a skill on your individual conference note sheets. To meet the objectives in this unit, students' writing should show a development of the characters with a clear plot and sequence of events.

Celebrate the end of this unit by publishing children's stories for everyone to read. This will encourage writers to do their best work and also helps to build a nurturing community of writers where every writer can take risks and know that his writing is valued. Children's published pieces could go in a basket to be placed in the class or school library so children may "check out" one another's books.

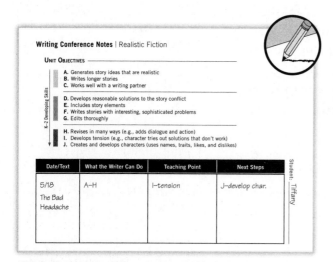

The final goal is for Tiffany to more fully develop the characters in her story

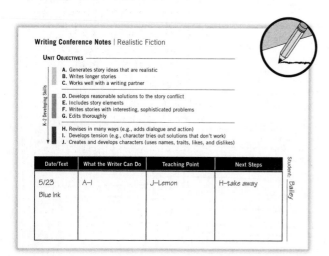

The teacher makes a note to work later on the more complex strategy of taking away unnecessary parts.

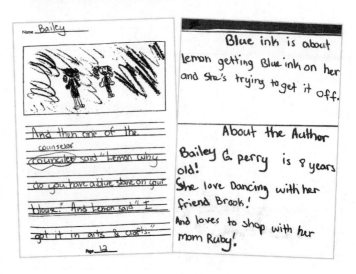

This second-grade writer clearly can write a quality piece that shows increasing length.

Many Kinds of Writing

Another unit that we generally cover with only kindergarten or first-grade students is one in which children try out various kinds of writing, like letters, lists, list books, signs, and songs. This unit works well at the beginning of the school year by exposing writers to a variety of genres before units focusing on narrative and nonnarrative writing. Children also learn that writing is purposeful and that they are writing for an audience. They may start off by labeling items in the classroom and creating signs for the school community, such as "Be quiet in the hallway."

It's a good idea to keep on hand several mentor texts that represent the diversity of writing you wish to familiarize your students with. *Carlo Likes Reading* by Jessica Spanyol (2001) is a good example of writing with labels. Highlight a page from *Our Granny* (1993) by Margaret Wild to show a model of a list. Remember to display examples of your own writing—supermarket lists, to-do lists, old cards you've received, and signs you've created. You can also type songs you've taught the class.

Lists are easy to generate quickly with young children, and the picture support that naturally goes with them helps make the piece easier to read.

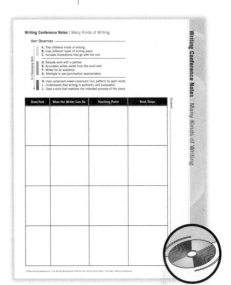

Objectives for Many Kinds of Writing unit
Print From CD/Copy From Appendix, page 108

ELL Tip

Labeling the classroom will help ELL students learn the necessary vocabulary to help them all year long. This unit helps build a common language for the classroom community. You could also work with a small group of students to label body parts by placing sticky notes on arms, legs, nose, forehead, and more. Labeling helps build important language skills. Letter writing helps to develop friendships within the classroom, which creates a risk-free environment. This builds the confidence and comfort level of English language learners.

This is a good example of a list created by a young student.

Sarah, a first grader, writes a get-well letter to her teacher.

A comic strip is a more advanced type of writing to try with second graders. In this sample, Yuria used a comic strip to relate a knock-knock joke.

Letters are also a fun format to introduce in the primary grades. They give children an audience to focus on for their writing. In the sample above, Sarah, a first-grade student, used all the proper conventions in this simple letter to her teacher (G). Her writing is purposeful (F, I), and shows good use of spelling strategies (E, H).

Students can celebrate throughout this unit by publishing their signs in a walk around the school community, publishing labels in the class-room, singing songs they created to their friends, and putting letters in friend's mailboxes. These quick projects are authentic and generate enthusiasm and excitement for the unit.

Taking a close look at student work gives you a lot of insight to use during assessment. The individualized Writing Conference Notes sheets, although brief, provide a window into what each student is capable of as well as where to go next in your instruction. The range of objectives for each unit allows you to differentiate your instruction to meet the needs of all the writers in your class.

Chapter 4

Conferring to Reach Writers at All Levels

"A mentor builds on strength, often seeing more in a student's work than the student sees."

RALPH FLETCHER, (1992) *WHAT A WRITER NEEDS*

As a new school year begins, you can expect to welcome students of all abilities into your classroom—children who are going to perform at grade level, children who need extra support, and children who have a good grasp of the content and need an additional challenge. In order to reach the range of abilities in your classroom, this chapter describes students at each grade level (K–2) at the beginning of the year.

In this chapter you will find answers to the following questions:

- What kinds of observations can I make?
- How do I analyze and prioritize the objectives?
- How can I differentiate assessment and instruction to help support all the writers in my classroom?
- How will the writers in my classroom grow as they advance through the primary grades?
- What might writing look like at the start of the school year?
- How can different conversations go as I confer with many levels of writers in my class?

Portrait of Writers Who Are Performing at Grade Level

Harshini has learned to draw details that describe the setting of her story.

Students who are performing at grade level in the fall have a good sense of story structure and presentation. They have focused on and absorbed and practiced storytelling, both in school and at home. They have a good knowledge of sight words and sound-letter correspondence, which help them write with ease, and they attempt to use grade-appropriate conventions.

Kindergarten writers can print the initial consonant for words, while students in first grade are able to write the initial and final consonants in words and may include simple sight words in their stories. Students in second grade use blends, vowels, and word endings in their words, and can generate story ideas, but may need a little push to produce several writing pieces across the unit of study.

SUPPORTING WRITERS WHO ARE PERFORMING AT GRADE LEVEL IN KINDERGARTEN

Kindergarteners are generally able to draw clear pictures with characters. They also tend to include basic setting details (like weather elements) in their illustrations. Some students attempt initial labeling for writing the names of characters, like "Mom" and "me." They may tell the teacher a simple story: "I went to park with Mom." Letter reversals are common, and children may struggle with writing their names clearly. Spacing between words is also difficult at this point.

Harshini begins kindergarten with the knowledge that stories have characters and a setting. She adds facial expressions to show that characters are happy and labels the characters with initial consonants. She knows her name starts with an /h/ sound so she labels it with an *h*. Because Harshini does not yet have a grasp of initial consonant sounds, she uses letter sounds she knows to help with labeling. She also experiments with the use of upper- and lowercase letters.

Based on these observations and the Unit 1 objectives, Harshini's teacher might choose to work on one of the following:

- Using initial consonant sounds to write a simple sentence to match the picture
- Choosing paper to allow for illustration and corresponding sentence(s)
- Adding more details in the illustration to add to the plot

Here's how a conference between Harshini and her teacher focusing on the teaching point of adding more details to the plot might go:

Ms. J: Great job getting started right away with writing workshop, Harshini. You even had time to label the characters in your story. Who are these people?

Harshini: That's me and my mom. See—"h" for Harshini!

Ms. J: Excellent! I also notice that it's a sunny day and there's lots of grass! Writers can tell more of a story by adding to the pictures. What is going on there?

Harshini: Mommy and me are walking through the garden. We look at flowers.

Ms. J: Oh...so what do you think you can add to the pictures to show me that?

Harshini: Maybe some flowers?

Ms. J: Great thinking! Remember to draw as much as you can to show me what's happening in your story when it's writing time!

(Harshini quickly starts to add different colored flowers to her paper.)

Writing Conference Notes | Launching the Writing Workshop

UNIT OBJECTIVES

K-2 Developing Skills

A. Understands and follows the routines of writing workshop (conferring)
B. Generates ideas for writing topics
C. Is able to tell a story (orally and written)

D. Cooperatively works with a writing partner
E. Able to complete the writing process in a timely manner
F. Writes labels and/or sentences
G. Chooses appropriate paper choice

H. Uses sound-letter correspondence
I. Uses a variety of spelling strategies
J. Revises by adding to the pictures, adding words or adding pages

Student: Harshini

Date/Text	What the Writer Can Do	Teaching Point	Next Steps
9/15	A—gets right to work F—labels people	C—tell more of story with details in pics	F/G—one line paper to add one sent.

In the next conference, the teacher will work with Harshini in adding a sentence to the story.

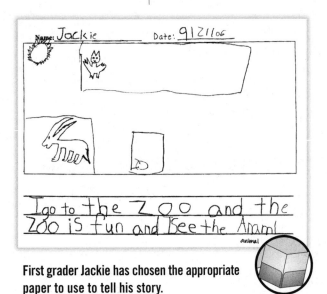

First grader Jackie has chosen the appropriate paper to use to tell his story.

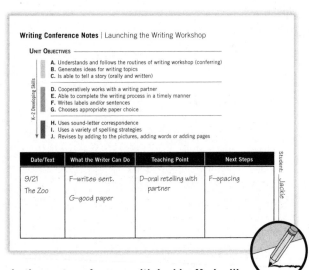

In the next conference with Jackie, Mr. L will focus on spacing between letters.

SUPPORTING WRITERS WHO ARE PERFORMING AT GRADE LEVEL IN FIRST GRADE

At the start of first grade, most students will be able to write simple one- to two-page stories. The plots are limited and the story ideas are often repetitive—one child's folder might contain several stories about going to the park or the zoo. They might use simple conventions like capital *I*. Writers at this stage often rely heavily on words they know how to spell, which limits how much detail their stories contain. Sometimes they try spelling a few unknown words by stretching them out. A kindergartener performing at grade level can write his initial and final consonants, and will attempt vowels, but lacks the knowledge to use them properly.

Jackie's story has a simple picture with matching text. He includes several sight words—*go*, *the*, and *see*—but uses inconsistent spacing. Based on these observations and the Unit 1 objectives, Jackie's teacher might choose to work on one of the following:

- Adding details to the story by using oral storytelling with a partner
- Limiting the use of *and* (using shorter sentences or other constructions)
- Punctuating
- Adding information to pictures before writing to generate more story details

Here's how a conference between Jackie and his teacher focusing on the first teaching point of oral storytelling with a partner might go:

Mr. L: What are you working on, Jackie?

Jackie: I go to zoo. Zoo is fun. I see the animal.

Mr. L: Oh... I see. I go to the zoo. The zoo is fun. I see all of the animals. I'm happy to see you tried writing sentences like authors do.

Jackie: I see the goat. I see the bear.

Mr. L: Oh, Jackie. You have more of a story to tell. A writer can tell his story to a partner to help him add more to the writing. It sounds like you may be ready for another page. Let's get a writing partner for you. Ethan, can you come here?

(Ethan walks over to the conference nook.)

Mr. L: I have great news! You two are going to be writing partners. When you think you are done with a story, I want you to tell the story to your partner first and see if you are missing any parts in your sentences. Jackie is ready to tell his story to you, Ethan.

(Jackie reads his piece and adds new parts. Ethan listens.)

Ethan: Hey, you didn't write about the bear and goat!

Jackie: Oh, yeah....

Ethan: Why don't you write that on this paper?

Jackie: Okay.

(Jackie takes the paper and writes: *I see bear and I see the goat.* Mr. L takes his notes on the conference note sheet at this time.)

SUPPORTING WRITERS WHO ARE PERFORMING AT GRADE LEVEL IN SECOND GRADE

At the beginning of second grade young writers include basic story elements in their writing. They may move away from the use of illustrations and want to focus on print. You may also see evidence of some revision strategies they've learned. By this time, students have come to appreciate the power of words—yet some might have a strong distaste for writing workshop and may need extra encouragement to come up with new and interesting story ideas. These students often focus on big events in their lives, such as special places they've visited, and benefit from small-group work on developing simple story ideas from their everyday lives.

Cathryn remembers to use sound words like *beep beep* to add interesting details. She also attempts dialogue and includes several characters in her piece. Based on these observations and the Unit 1 objectives, Cathryn's teacher might choose to work on one of the following:

- Using revision strategies such as adding internal thinking and body actions
- Illustrating the scene to help add to the words of the story

Here's how a conference between Cathryn and her teacher focusing on the second teaching point might go:

Mrs. B: Oh Cathryn...I love birthdays too! Writing about birthday parties is fun! I see that you remembered from last year how to add sound words to your story, like *beep beep*.

Cathryn: Yeah, Ms. C taught us that!

> Birthday Time
>
> I went to my aunt's house on Sunday. I was able to hear the cars beeping outside - beep beep. It was a birthday party. We all sang "Happy Birthday to you" Everyone was laughing -ha ha ha. Anthony Opend up his gifs and was very happy. He said "thankyou to everyone.

Second grader Cathryn chooses a topic that is meaningful to her—a cousin's birthday.

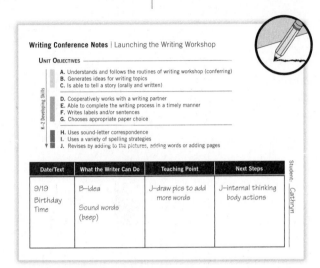

Writing Conference Notes | Launching the Writing Workshop

UNIT OBJECTIVES

A. Understands and follows the routines of writing workshop (conferring)
B. Generates ideas for writing topics
C. Is able to tell a story (orally and written)

D. Cooperatively works with a writing partner
E. Able to complete the writing process in a timely manner
F. Writes labels and/or sentences
G. Chooses appropriate paper choice

H. Uses sound-letter correspondence
I. Uses a variety of spelling strategies
J. Revises by adding to the pictures, adding words or adding pages

Date/Text	What the Writer Can Do	Teaching Point	Next Steps
9/19 Birthday Time	B–idea Sound words (beep)	J–draw pics to add more words	J–internal thinking body actions

Student: Cathryn

Later, Mrs. B will encourage Cathryn to revise to show a character's internal thinking and his or her body movement.

Mrs. B: Great! So Anthony got lots of presents at his party, huh?

Cathryn: Yeah, he got racing cars and Twister, and I got him checkers.

Mrs. B: Why don't you draw a quick sketch of the birthday party and show that?

Here's some blank paper to sketch on.

(Cathryn begins to draw the birthday party. Mrs. B quickly jots her conference notes as Cathryn draws.)

Mrs. B: Let's look at your picture carefully. Is there anything from your picture that can help you add to your words?

Cathryn: Umm…I could write the presents he got.

Mrs. B: Sounds like a plan! So next time you can sketch and use your drawing to help you add to the words in your story.

Portrait of Writers Who Need More Support

Some children start the school year with a very limited knowledge of how to write a story. These students need intensive small-group instruction as well as support in individual conferences to help them master the unit objectives. It's important to assess all your students in September through conferences as well as by examining their work to determine the support that they'll need.

In the first unit, you launch the writing workshop. In the following months, narrative writing will be the focus. This sequence allows ample time to expose students to a variety of narratives and for them to understand that all writers have stories to tell about their lives.

SUPPORTING STRUGGLING WRITERS IN KINDERGARTEN

Some children entering kindergarten may have never written stories before. They might start out the year with scribbles or pictures of things they know how to draw. These students will probably not write labels or sentences, and their illustrations may not have a story behind them. When asked about their work, they may be unsure of what their story is about. They may be unable to write their name, and they may be unsure where their name belongs on the paper.

Jahira has begun the year in kindergarten by drawing pictures with few details. She draws the bodies of the characters loosely. The paper is upside down with the name in the wrong place. She has difficulty spelling her name as well. Clearly, Jahira needs more support in setting up her page for |writing before her teacher tackles any skills related to story writing. Based on these observations and the Unit 1 objectives, Jahira's teacher might choose to work on one of the following:

- Writing her name correctly
- Telling stories orally
- Representational drawing in small group instruction
- Reteaching of previous objectives

Here's how a conference between Jahira and her teacher focusing on the teaching point of writing her name and the date correctly might go:

Ms. P: Good morning, Jahira. Wow. I see you've been working hard in writing workshop today. Can you tell me about your piece?

(Jahira doesn't say anything. She points to the paper.)

Ms. P: I see all the characters on your paper. Great job trying to draw the people in your story. Is that your family?

Jahira: Yeah, Mommy, Daddy, brother, me.

(Ms. P takes out her personal writing folder and pulls out her model piece from the mini-lesson she taught the previous day.)

Ms. P: Jahira, do you remember how I wrote about going to the park yesterday? Here it is. And look—I used the same paper that you did. Well, I want to show you how you can write your name and stamp your date in the right spot on your paper.

(Ms. P shows her piece to Jahira and points out where the name and date belong.)

Ms. P: Do you see where it says "Name" and "Date?" Right next to it, I wrote "Ms. P" for my name and stamped the date. Then I drew my picture below it.

Jahira: Yeah, can I do that too?

Ms. P: Sure. Look at your writing. Can you turn the paper and point out where your name belongs?

Jahira, a kindergartner, has turned her paper upside down and written her name on the sentence line.

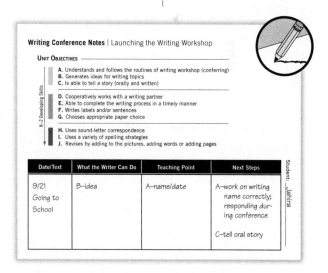

Ms. P writes a detailed note to guide her work with Jahira on objective A for the next conference.

Jahira: Here.

Ms. P: Great! Now show me where you would stamp the date.

Jahira: I know. (She points to the correct place on the paper.)

Ms. P: I see you're about to start a new piece of writing. Why don't you take a new piece of paper and show me how to write your name and stamp the date in the right place?

(Jahira gets a new piece of paper and follows through on what the teacher has asked of her. While she's doing that, Ms. P jots the conference notes shown on page 77. Ms. P quickly glances over to check on Jahira before beginning to confer with another student.)

This first grade writer relies exclusively on visual details to tell his story.

SUPPORTING STRUGGLING WRITERS IN FIRST GRADE

In September, first graders who need extra help might have a sense of story but they lack the ability to tell a story effectively. They may be able to do some oral storytelling but have trouble translating stories into writing. These students often rely heavily on drawing pictures and use details in their pictures to provide insight into what the story is about. They may write simple sentences based on their sight-word knowledge.

Salomon begins the year engrossed in his imagination. His picture clearly shows a story idea with lots of setting details—including weather. Though he can tell his story orally, Salomon doesn't attempt to tell his story in simple sentences. Based on these observations and the Unit 1 objectives, Salomon's teacher might choose to work on one of the following:

- Labeling the pictures
- Extending the labels into simple sentences
- Spelling strategies in a small-group setting that include the use of the class word wall
- Generating a shared-writing piece

Here's how a conference between Salomon and his teacher focusing on the first two teaching points might go:

Ms. C: Hi, Salomon. It looks like you have a lot going on in your story. What's happening here?

Salomon: I went to amusement park, lots of rides and things to do. It was fun.

Ms. C: Great job telling me about your story. You sure have a lot to say. Great writers also try to write words to go with their pictures. Do you see the lines at the bottom of the page? What do you think goes there?

Salomon: The story.

Ms. C: Right. You told me you went to an amusement park. Let's try to write that here.

(Ms. C points to the lines and repeats the story Salomon has told her. She taps at the lines and points to the space where he should write them. Salomon picks up his pencil and writes *I*.)

Ms. C: Great start with the words. Keep it up, and I'll take a look at what you've done at the end of writing workshop. Why don't you share your piece today?

Salomon: Okay.

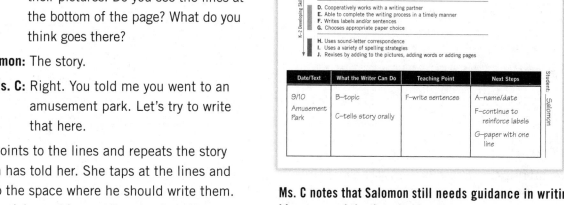

Ms. C notes that Salomon still needs guidance in writing his name and the date on his paper.

SUPPORTING STRUGGLING WRITERS IN SECOND GRADE

Second graders tend to have some knowledge of how stories look in print and sound, but some children can only write very simple stories with few words and have trouble including details. These children often struggle to come up with a topic and because they are not yet using conventional spelling, they may spend a lot of time attempting to write words, which limits the quantity and quality of their work. Such children need additional support from you.

In the fall, Emily is able to choose a story idea and draw a scene with many details, but she writes only a small moment and struggles with adding details to her writing. Based on these observations and the Unit 1 objectives, Emily's teacher might choose to work on one of the following:

- Implementing story elements, such as developing the setting
- Adding details by using revision strategies
- Choosing the appropriate paper to tell the story
- Writing longer stories with three- and five-page writing booklets

Here's how a conference between Emily and her teacher focusing on the third teaching point might go:

The Whistler
"Hoooo" Adrian whistled in school
I whisped "You'r not allowed to
whistle in school" I said. But
Adrian didn't listen to me but he
didn't get cot.

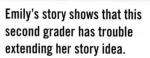

Emily's story shows that this second grader has trouble extending her story idea.

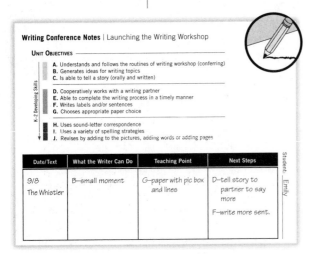

Date/Text	What the Writer Can Do	Teaching Point	Next Steps
9/8 The Whistler	B—small moment	G—paper with pic box and lines	D—tell story to partner to say more F—write more sent.

Student: Emily

In upcoming conferences, Mr. P will encourage Emily to extend her story by sharing it with a partner and help her to write more sentences in future stories.

Mr. P: Emily, I read your piece, and I love the simple idea you chose of Adrian whistling. Stories can be about anything! Do you remember where you can find paper in our classroom?

Emily: Sure. It's in the back in the writing center. (She points to it.)

Mr. P: Right, there are a lot of different types of paper to choose from. Writers choose paper to help them write their best story. When you are about to begin to write, it's a good idea to take a moment and look at the different kinds of paper to choose from. Let's go take a look!

(They walk to the writing center.)

Mr. P: Do you see the paper over here? (He points to paper with a picture box and several lines below.)

Emily: Yeah. I never used that before!

Mr. P: Well, how might your story go on here?

(Emily retells her story by touching the lined portion of the page. Then she points to the box above the lines.)

Emily: And I could draw a picture here!

Mr. P: Yes, you could. Do you have an idea for your next story?

Emily: I was going to write about playing tag at recess.

Mr. P: Sounds like another good idea. Let's plan how that story might go on this paper!

(Emily tells the story to herself and points to the picture space as she describes how she would draw a picture of her friends playing tag.)

Mr. P: Sounds like you're going to choose better paper for your story this time around. Let's see how it goes, and remember—when you want to start a new story, you can make a plan first to help you choose the right paper.

Portrait of Writers Who Are Ready for an Additional Challenge

Some writers begin the school year with a great sense of story. Many of them love writing workshop and consider it the best time of the day. These young writers are often proficient readers who read for long periods of time. They draw on their vivid imaginations when writing stories, and because writing feels easy for them, they greatly enjoy doing it. Spelling usually doesn't seem overly important to these students so they don't tend to get hung up on unknown words. This allows them to freely explore a variety of words, which helps to build the quality of their work. Their work tends to show the beginnings of an authentic writer's voice.

SUPPORTING WRITERS WHO ARE READY FOR AN ADDITIONAL CHALLENGE IN KINDERGARTEN

Kindergarten students may feel confident in their ability to draw, which allows them to add details to their illustrations. They may even attempt to draw from a variety of angles to show specific information that is important to their stories. Their work often includes labels and sometimes simple sentences as well. These children have a good pencil grasp and often know how to correctly form letters of the alphabet. They understand the purpose of writing workshop and realize that words and pictures convey a message.

Kirin quickly gets to work when it's writing workshop time. She is able to draw from the profile perspective and includes frontal views as well. She also uses spaces and punctuation, and demonstrates knowledge of high-frequency words in her simple sentence. Based on these observations and the Unit 1 objectives, Kirin's teacher might choose to work on one of the following:

- Using a personal word wall
- Choosing paper with lines to encourage multi-event stories
- Writing across several pages in small booklets
- Developing the plot

Here's how a conference between Kirin and her teacher focusing on the teaching point of using a personal word wall might go:

Mr. S: Kirin, why don't we take a look in your folder and see some writing you've done.

Kirin: Look Mr. S! Remember our trip to Pathmark? I wrote about that.

Mr. S: Wow! I love how you labeled your picture and wrote a sentence too.

Kirin: That was a fun trip.

Mr. S: Yes, it was! You know so many words, but I see here that you spelled the word *was* with a *z*. Today I'm going to give you a special chart that has a lot of words that you'll be using in writing workshop. This

Kirin, a kindergartner, uses labels in her drawing to convey meaning.

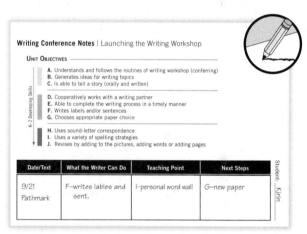

Mr. S notes that Kirin is ready to go on to choose paper that will enable her to tell a multi-event story.

will be your own personal word wall that you can keep in your writing folder. When you're not sure about a word, you can just take it out and look for the word so you can spell it correctly.

Kirin: Cool!

Mr. S: So, Kirin, can you find the word *was* on the word wall?

(Kirin looks carefully through the list of words. She stops and points to the correct word.)

Mr. S: Good work! Now you can go back and spell the word correctly. Remember to use the word wall whenever you're unsure of a word.

SUPPORTING WRITERS WHO ARE READY FOR AN ADDITIONAL CHALLENGE IN FIRST GRADE

First graders needing a challenge might start off the year writing booklets. They may write across many pages and request additional paper so they can expand their work. Their stories contain a plot with characters, a problem, and a solution. Pictures match the words, and students may add speech bubbles to their illustrations. These writers often show expressions on their character's faces. They have a bank of simple sight words to use in their writing, and they understand that their work will be read by others. These children use their knowledge of word families and word endings to spell words.

First grader Naya writes about a moment when she needed her mom.

Naya writes across several pages and creates spacing slashes throughout her piece so it's easier to read—a technique that shows an advanced knowledge of editing. The facial expressions of the characters change across the pages, showing the development of feelings. Based on these observations and the Unit 1 objectives, Naya's teacher might choose to work on one of the following:

- Writing conventions like capitalization and punctuation
- Spelling strategies such as spelling patterns and blends
- Extending dialogue into the text

Here's how a conference between Naya and her teacher focusing on the teaching point with objective I might go:

Ms. S: We're getting ready to publish, so it's time to edit, Naya. I see that you help your reader by using slashes for spaces. That really helps me read your piece. Another way to edit is to use the word wall in our class to help us spell sight words correctly. Let's touch each word as we read your piece and see if there are any word wall words. I'll do the first line.

(Ms. S begins to read the piece and stops at the word *wuz*.)

Ms. S: Hmmm . . . "wuz." I think this word is on the word wall. Let me go check.

(Ms. S walks over to the word wall, finds the word *was* on a sticky note, peels it off the wall, and brings it back to Naya's seat.)

Ms. S: Oh look! I found it! Let me check if the word is spelled correctly.

(Ms. S compares the sticky note to the written word. She crosses out the word and corrects it above.)

Ms. S: Did you see how I used the word wall to help with spelling? Why don't you read on and see if you find any other words that we can check?

Naya: All right.

(Naya continues to touch each word and read it aloud. She stops at *win* and goes to the word wall. She retrieves the *when* sticky note. She looks it over and edits the word.)

Ms. S: Great job editing with the word wall. Keep it up!

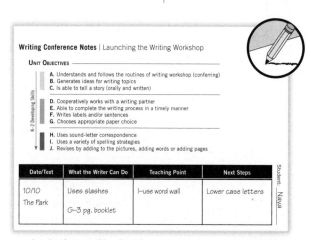

In the future, Ms. S will concentrate on helping Naya understand the rules for using lowercase letters in her sentences.

Supporting Writers Who Are Ready for an Additional Challenge in Second Grade

Second graders who are ready for a greater challenge might have lengthy stories that showcase all the author crafts they've learned in previous grades. These techniques include dialogue, show-not-tell, internal thinking, tension, and character action. Special punctuation like ellipses, commas, and quotation marks may be evident. These children often have a large vocabulary that shows up in the text. In order to differentiate to meet their needs, you can use mentor texts to teach special craft elements; students can work in a small group around a mentor text of your choosing. They may be ready to learn the proper way to use advanced punctuation, like commas. Students can also work with a partner to help their story move along. Reading their pieces regularly to a partner who is also ready for a challenge can provide support for both students.

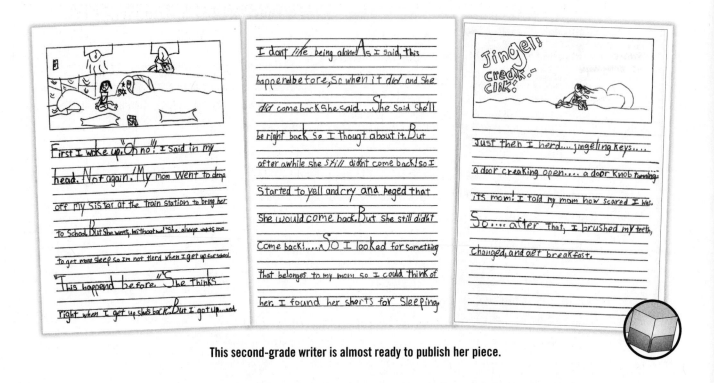

This second-grade writer is almost ready to publish her piece.

Although it's the start of the year, Madison needs a challenge to help take her writing to the next level. Listening to whole-class lessons will not provide the support she needs. Her piece shows a strong voice and includes a great plot line. There is dialogue, action, internal thinking, and suspense. Madison attempts a variety of punctuation marks, including ellipses, exclamation marks, commas, and quotation marks. Her pictures are detailed and thoroughly support her words. Based on these observations and the Unit 1 objectives, Madison's teacher might choose to work on one of the following:

- Word-solving strategies to improve her spelling
- Adding word endings
- Investigating words to come up with generalizations about them

Here's how a conference between Madison and her teacher focusing on the teaching point might go:

Madison: Hi, Ms. A! Look at my work!

(Ms. A reads Madison's piece.)

> **Ms. A:** Madison, you've got so much voice in your writing. It sounds like you're talking right to me.

Madison: I know!

> **Ms. A:** Are you going to publish this piece?

Madison: Yeah!

> **Ms. A:** Let me teach you a new spelling rule to help you with editing. Remember when we were learning about verbs that end in *–ed*? We made a chart of words that end with *–ed*. Sometimes they sound like *d*, *t*, or *ed*. Let's read your piece and see if any words sound that way at the end. Then you can make sure you end the word with *–ed*.

(Madison looks over her piece and corrects the words *tierd* and *happend*.)

> **Ms. A:** From now on, think carefully when spelling the endings of words.

Madison: That's a good idea, Ms. A!

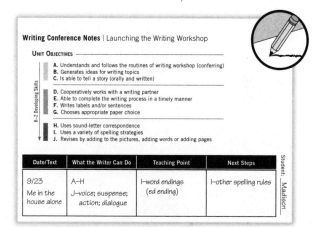

Writing Conference Notes | Launching the Writing Workshop

UNIT OBJECTIVES

K–2 Developing Skills

A. Understands and follows the routines of writing workshop (conferring)
B. Generates ideas for writing topics
C. Is able to tell a story (orally and written)

D. Cooperatively works with a writing partner
E. Able to complete the writing process in a timely manner
F. Writes labels and/or sentences
G. Chooses appropriate paper choice

H. Uses sound-letter correspondence
I. Uses a variety of spelling strategies
J. Revises by adding to the pictures, adding words or adding pages

Student: Madison

Date/Text	What the Writer Can Do	Teaching Point	Next Steps
9/23 Me in the house alone	A–H J–voice; suspense; action; dialogue	I–word endings (ed ending)	I–other spelling rules

As Ms. A notes in her assessment, Madison shows mastery of almost all the objectives for the unit.

No classroom is composed of a homogeneous group of students who consistently perform at the same level. Some students will achieve grade-level expectations. Others will fall short of those goals, while others will be ready to meet additional academic challenges. Recording your students' progress on your conference notes will allow you to differentiate the assessment in your writing workshop so you'll be able to meet the needs of all children.

Chapter 5

Improving Assessment, Planning, and Teaching with Data-Collection Tools

"Conferences are important, but now we've learned to place them in a different context. More important, we've learned much more about the essentials of teaching writing and how to use our time more effectively."

DONALD H. GRAVES, (1994) *A FRESH LOOK AT WRITING*

Before beginning any unit, planning is key. It's important to reflect on previous units of study, think about units to come, and consider student successes and difficulties.

In this chapter you will find answers to the following questions:

- What tools might help me plan my own units and what kind of data can I collect with them?
- How might I use checklists within my own classroom to support writing workshop?
- How can my conference notes help me confer with the writers in my classroom next time?
- How can my assessments inform small-group instruction?
- How can my conference notes assist me in planning strategy lessons?

Making the Most of the Data You Collect

The information you collect from conferences can be very useful for planning your curriculum and instruction. As you look over your notes periodically, you may notice patterns within your classroom. These patterns can help you guide upcoming lessons and target areas where students need the most support. Several tools can help you collect and organize this data: the Writing Conference Notes sheet, different versions of the Planning Form sheet, and the Class Checklist sheet. (You'll find these forms on the companion CD and in the Appendix on pages 106–143.) We've introduced these tools in previous chapters and will explore them more here.

WRITING CONFERENCE NOTES SHEET

The Writing Conference Notes sheets are designed to help you take shorthand, easy-to-review notes that allow you to track objectives for the entire year, unit by unit. Because the objectives you teach may change based on the needs of the students within your classroom, it's helpful to reflect on the goals of the previous unit before you begin a new one. Ask yourself the following question: *Have students met the goals I set for them?* If they still have not mastered some skills, you may wish to revise the Writing Conference Notes sheet for the next unit to include these skills in the Unit Objectives list at the top of the sheet. You may also think about additional objectives you'd like to accomplish during a unit of study and add these to the list. This will help guide you in developing an appropriate set of skills for the unit objectives.

Writing Conference Notes
Print From CD/Copy From Appendix, page 117

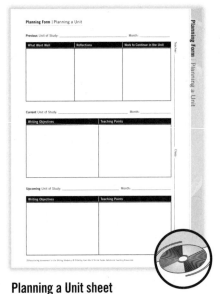

Planning a Unit sheet
Print From CD/Copy From Appendix,
page 130

After filling out a planning form, Ms. W can see clearly how her units will develop.

A blank Writing Conference Notes sheet like the one shown on page 87 can serve as a tool for you to develop student-specific goals for your units of study and create units that we haven't addressed. You can also differentiate or level the goals to meet the specific needs of your students. For example, a second-grade student who is new to this country may struggle to express himself in writing. You may wish to start him off with the simpler goal of labeling people and objects in his illustrations while your more proficient writers are working on adding more pages to their stories.

Planning Forms

Different Planning Forms can assist you in preparing a unit of your own creation: Planning a Unit, Planning a Mini-Lesson, and Strategy Group Sheet.

As you plan a new unit, take a few moments to analyze how successful your students have been at mastering the previous unit's objectives. Ask yourself the following questions: *What went well during my last unit of study? Which goals did students struggle to accomplish? Which objectives do students need more practice in?*

On the Planning a Unit form, list your writing objectives for the next unit of study in order of increasing difficulty, and then use the notes on your planning sheet to help you complete a blank Writing Conference Notes sheet. Your unit of study will go much more smoothly as a result. At left is a sample of a planning sheet filled out by a second-grade teacher.

For a discussion of using the Planning a Mini-Lesson sheet, see page 95. See pages 91–93 for information on the Strategy Group Sheet planning form.

Class Checklist Sheet

Looking at 20 or more conference note sheets can be overwhelming and confusing. It's also difficult to carry so many forms around with you, which is why Class Checklist sheets can become a helpful organizational tool. The checklist helps you keep track of how the class is doing as a whole, and it highlights patterns of learning within your classroom. This data will enable you to differentiate lessons to meet all students' needs. (Refer to Chapter 1, pages 22–23 for more information on how to use checklists successfully in your classroom.)

Using Your Notes for Future Conferences

Before you start to confer with a child, look at the last few Writing Conference Notes sheets you've completed for that student.

The teacher glances at her previous conference notes on this student to help guide her conference.

Look over at the teaching points section, and notice whether the student is now successfully implementing the objectives you taught in your teaching point. If, in fact, this young writer is meeting those objectives, compliment her on her success. If difficulties are still apparent, you may need to reteach the skill during the next conference. You may also decide on teaching points for your next conference with this student by looking at the notes you've made in the Next Steps section. Any objectives that the student has not yet mastered can become future teaching points during conference time. Of course, the student's current writing will also serve as a guide for future conferences.

Let's put conferring preparation in action and prepare for a future conference with Jackie, a first grader who was performing at grade level during the launching unit of writing workshop (See Chapter 4: Portrait of Writers Who Are Performing at Grade Level, pages 74–75.) A glance at Jackie's September 21 Writing Conference Notes sheet can give his teacher an indication of what to focus on for the next conference.

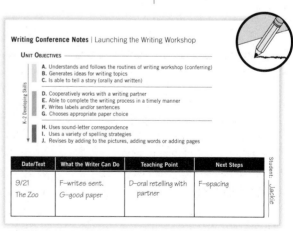

Jackie needs some help with objective F, so his teacher will probably work with him on the spacing between words.

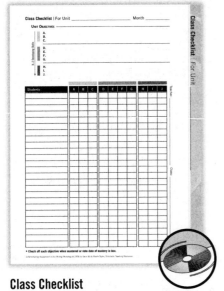

Class Checklist

Print From CD/Copy From Appendix, page 128

Jackie worked on retelling his story to his partner at the previous meeting (D). In this conference, the teacher will check to see how Jackie is doing with this skill. If Jackie has mastered it he'll compliment him on the partner work. Then the teacher might work on spacing (F) with Jackie, since he recorded that objective in the Next Steps section. However, if Jackie isn't yet able to retell a story to his partner, the teacher may wish to revisit this teaching point. It's crucial that students achieve the objectives in a variety of their writing pieces.

You may also want to consult your Class Checklist sheet before making any conferring decisions. The sample below is for class 1-113, Jackie's first-grade class.

Class 1-113's checklist sheet for September's writing unit shows that Jackie isn't the only student in the class experiencing partnership difficulties. Since most of the class is struggling with this skill, the teacher might find it helpful to teach a whole-class mini-lesson on this topic. Addressing these skills with the whole class can save valuable conferring time. If Jackie still struggles with partnerships after the rest of the class is beginning to master it, his teacher may wish to revisit this objective during conference time.

The Class Checklist shows clearly which objectives students are having difficulty mastering.

Class Checklist | Launching the Writing Workshop

UNIT OBJECTIVES

K–2 Developing Skills

A. Understands and follows the routines of writing workshop (conferring)
B. Generates ideas for writing topics
C. Is able to tell a story (orally and written)

D. Cooperatively works with a writing partner
E. Able to complete the writing process in a timely manner
F. Writes labels and/or sentences
G. Chooses appropriate paper choice

H. Uses sound-letter correspondence
I. Uses a variety of spelling strategies
J. Revises by adding to the pictures, adding words or adding pages

Teacher: Stevens   Class: 1-113

Students	A	B	C	D	E	F	G	H	I	J
Taren	9/6	9/6	9/11	9/6		9/18	9/11		9/18	9/11
Mike R.	9/6		9/6			9/22				
Patrick		9/7	9/14	9/7			9/7			
Ammar	9/4	9/4	9/14			9/20			9/20	
Tony	9/5		9/11							
Derek	9/4	9/4				9/27	9/7			9/7
Emily	9/20	9/20				9/18				
Caitlyn	9/13	9/17	9/22	9/13		9/22				
Samantha	9/14				9/22	9/14				
Bonnie	9/11	9/19	9/11			9/19			9/11	9/11
Ryan	9/6	9/6	9/21			9/21				
Vivian	9/8	9/8	9/25			9/15				
Bryan	9/8		9/18	9/8		9/28				
Mike C.	9/7	9/7	9/18	9/7		9/26				
Alex	9/5	9/5	9/5			9/5	9/15	9/3		9/13
Keith	9/20	9/20	9/20	9/20		9/8				
Caroline	9/8	9/15	9/8			9/22				
Nicole	9/15	9/19		9/19		9/19				
Roy	9/13	9/5	9/5							
Navjeet	9/8	9/8			9/15					
Emra	9/6		9/27							
Melissa		9/19				9/19				
Joy		9/12	9/12			9/20				
Jennifer	9/13	9/19	9/20	9/20					9/12	
Esther	9/7	9/7				9/13				
Jackie	9/15	9/15	9/6			9/21	9/21			

Using Your Notes for Small-Group Instruction

When a handful of children in your class are not mastering a particular objective, you can fit small-group work into the independent writing time of your workshop, allowing 10 to 15 minutes for a group of four to six children. Although you won't be able to confer with as many individuals on the days that you do small-group work, this instruction will serve as conference time for the children in your group. Your Class Checklist sheets help you sort out students for grouping: When you notice four to six blank spaces in a particular column, then it may be time to form a strategy group.

Another look at class 1-113's checklist sheet reveals that small groups of students are having trouble with the following skills: coming up with ideas for writing (B), telling a story (orally and in writing) (C), and writing labels (F). These groups of children would benefit from meeting with you in small-group settings, where you can review material, terms, and ideas you've covered in whole-group instruction and individual conferences.

Following your note-taking protocol for conferences, you'll use a Strategy Group Sheet (shown at right), to take notes during strategy group sessions. These will serve as conference notes and help you keep track of which students you've met with and which skills you've targeted. After each session, mark the dates on the Conference Dates Checklist sheet for the students with whom you met.

As you take notes on the Strategy Group Sheet, remember to record the skill letter that you are working on in the space beside Unit Objective. You can then be more specific about the skill you are teaching. For example, if you are working on objective C, telling a story (orally), you may teach students how to draw pictures that will support them as they tell the beginning, middle, and end or their story. Keep in mind that you may have to reinforce the skill several times with the same group of children. Therefore, you may use different tools for each lesson. For instance, to teach children how to orally tell a story with a writing partner, you may have another teacher act as your writing partner and prompt you, or invite a former student who knows how to be a good writing partner. Recording the tool used will help you if you need to reteach and vary your approach.

Tip

Students' grade level and where their skills fall on the continuum are important considerations. For example, children in first grade are not expected to meet objectives H–J. Therefore, small-group work focusing on these objectives may not be necessary unless they are ready for enrichment and small-group work in these areas.

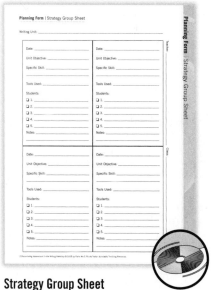

Strategy Group Sheet
Print From CD/Copy From Appendix, page 132

Some objectives that will require small-group instruction are easy to anticipate. For example, every year during the Launching the Writing Workshop unit, several children never fail to complain that they can't come up with writing ideas, objective B. As the Class Checklist on page 90 shows, class 1-113 is typical: Mike R., Tony, Samantha, Brian, and Emra, are struggling with developing ideas for writing workshop. Because the skill is complex, these students may need several small-group lessons before they get a handle on initiating their own writing.

Take a look at how one small-group lesson led by Mr. S might go:

(Mr. S calls the children to a meeting area. He asks them to bring their writing folders and pencils. The rest of the students are writing independently at their seats.)

Mr. S: Boys and girls, I called all of you here because I know how much you care about writing workshop. You want to make the most of your writing time, but all of you have told me that you're having trouble coming up with story ideas. That happens to a lot of writers. It's called "writer's block." Real writers learn ways to stop their writer's block so they can start writing. One way to come up with story ideas is to think about important people in your lives. Let's take a minute to think about all the important people in our lives.

(Mr. S pauses and allows children to think for a moment. He writes "Important Kinds of People in Our Lives" on chart paper.)

Mr. S: So, I was thinking about the important kinds of people in my life, and I came up with my students. They are important to me, and I could come up with a lot of stories about them. Let me write the word *students* on our chart.

(Mr. S shows them the chart and records *students*.)

Mr. S: So, what other ideas do you have to add to our chart?

Emra: How about family? My mom is important!

Mike: ...and my dad!

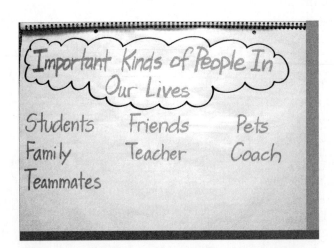

Hanging the chart in the writing center gives all the children access to the writing ideas recorded on it.

Tony: And my friends? Like Tommy. One time, we went to the park.

Samantha: Yeah, also my teachers. I love to write about them!

Brian: I play soccer! How about coaches and teammates?

Mr. S: Wow! You sure came up with a lot of ideas. I'm going to add them to the chart while you begin writing about one of these important people. I can't wait to read your stories! So, the next time you have writer's block, remember that you can write about important people in your lives. You can always check the chart for help. I'm going to put it in the writing center.

(Mr. S sends off the students, who enthusiastically begin to write. He later completes the chart and hangs it in the writing center for viewing.)

Mr. S has prepared in advance for his strategy group. While he was planning his approach for teaching this objective, he filled in the top portion of the Strategy Group Sheet (see below), and this sheet became his lesson plan for the mini-lesson.

He continues to use the Strategy Group Sheet to record notes for the six students in this group. After Mr. S sends the children off to write, he confers with another student and then circulates around the room to check on how his small group is doing. If they have found a writing topic and have begun to write, he records the titles of the pieces they are writing and puts a checkmark next to each student's name.

**Planning Form	Strategy Group Sheet**		
Writing Unit: _Launching the Writing Workshop_		Teacher:
Date: _Sept. 22_	Date: _____	
Unit Objective: _B_	Unit Objective: _____	
Specific Skill: _Generating story ideas_	Specific Skill: _____	
Tools Used: _chart w/ important people_	Tools Used: _____	
Students:	Students:	
☑1. _Mike R.—My Dad_	☐1. _____	
☑2. _Tony—Tommy and me at the park_	☐2. _____	
☑3. _Samantha—Mr. Perez_	☐3. _____	
☑4. _Brian—Soccer Time_	☐4. _____	
☑5. _Emma—My Mom_	☐5. _____	
Notes: _____	Notes: _____	

Mr. S will monitor the group's progress and note it on the Strategy Group Sheet.

Using Your Notes for Whole-Group Instruction

Your decision to plan a whole-group lesson can be based on what you're noticing on your Class Checklist sheet. When you notice that most students have empty boxes for certain unit objectives, and you have already attempted to check this objective, you'll need to reteach it at least once. Consider approaching the lesson in a different way. For example, if you used a mentor text the first time you taught the skill, the next time you may want to try a student sample. Or if students have already talked to their neighbor for active engagement time, you may want to try having students reread their work.

Another look at the Class Checklist sheet for class 1-113 shows us that most students are still having trouble working with a writing partner (D). Let's assume Mr. S has attempted to teach this objective to the whole class. In the first lesson, he had a former student model helpful partnership behaviors with him in front of the class. This approach didn't work, and most students are still unsure what writing partnerships are. Mr. S considers what he might do to help students understand partner work better. He realizes that many children in his class this year are visual learners and decides to create a chart to show what he expects partners to do. This how-to chart will reinforce the steps he hopes partners will take during writing workshop. After this second lesson, he'll assess whether students are working more effectively as partners, mark the Class Checklist sheet, and determine whether to reteach the whole group, work with small groups, or address the needs of individual students in conferences.

The Class Checklist sheet really helps teachers quickly decide what to do next. It serves as a quick reference tool and minimizes planning time.

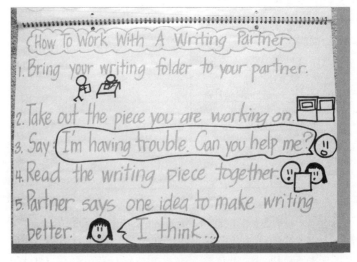

To help visual learners, include illustrations for the steps in a process.

PLANNING A MINI-LESSON SHEET

As you plan a mini-lesson, you want to be sure you consider all its components (see Chapter 2, pages 26–29.) The Planning a Mini-Lesson sheet below helps you address all the key lesson components and organize your ideas.

It provides several different options for how to approach your connection, teaching point, and active engagement. The completed planning sheet below shows how one kindergarten teacher planned her lesson on oral storytelling.

Now the teacher has a record of how she approached this lesson and how she can try a different connection, approach, or active engagement strategy if she needs to reteach the objective. The Planning a Mini-Lesson sheet reminds you of the many options you have at hand.

Planning Your Mini-lesson Sheet
Print From CD/Copy From Appendix, page 131

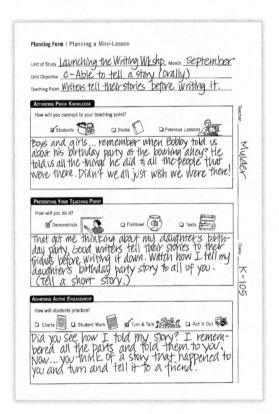

The teacher jots down specific examples to present to students.

Using these tools in concert will enable you to target key skills to teach and reteach in a timely way. Your conference notes and checklists are daily reminders of areas in which students are succeeding and need support. With this information, you can more effectively plan differentiated instruction for individuals, small groups, and the whole class.

Chapter 6

Using Your Conference Notes to Communicate About Student Achievement

"Parents are often very willing to help out—once they know we need it."

SHARON TABERSKI, (2000) *ON SOLID GROUND: STRATEGIES FOR TEACHING READING K–3*

When you have compiled conference notes on the strengths and areas of concern for the writers in your class, you will be better able to share this information with the student, their parents, your school support staff, and administrators. It's important to let them know which strategies and structures the child has in place and which ones he or she needs to continue to strive toward achieving.

In this chapter you will find answers to the following questions:

- How do I use my notes to communicate with my students?
- How do I use my notes to communicate with parents?
- How do I use my notes to communicate with school staff?
- How do I use my notes to communicate with administration?
- How might these conversations sound?

Using Your Assessments to Discuss and Support Student Achievement

When conferring is a consistent part of your writing instruction, students come to anticipate these conferences and pay attention to the notes that you take and share with them. In fact, these notes encourage accountability among the writers in your class. Students begin to realize that you will refer to your notes and check back to see if they are using the strategies that you've taught them.

Writers are more likely to try out the strategies when they think you are going to look at their work again in the future. They are writing for an audience, and their teacher becomes part of that audience. To help writers remember the strategies you've discussed at a conference, you can jot a reminder on a sticky note and place it in their writing folder. For kindergarteners and first graders, you can draw illustrations on the reminder. The illustrations help convey the essence of the strategy for those who may have difficulty reading.

This student looks on as the teacher jots down her conference notes. He knows what to expect.

This sticky note from a conference reminds the writer about questions she can ask herself that will help her add details to her story as she works independently in the future.

The teacher dates the sticky note.

These sticky notes serve as reminders and help you communicate your conference notes clearly to students. In the dialogue below, Ms. D reminds a young writer to refer to the sticky note so he can continue to use a blends chart as a spelling strategy.

(Ms. D confers with Timmy about his writing. She notices he often has difficulty spelling the beginning of words he doesn't know. Having noted this area of need on Timmy's conference note sheet, Ms. D decides to give Timmy a blends chart to keep in his folder and refer to when he's writing.)

Ms. D: Hi, Timmy. How's your writing going today?

Timmy: Great! I'm almost done with this story about Great Adventure. It was so much fun! I can't wait to go back!

Ms. D: That's terrific! Can you read your piece to me?

(Timmy reads his work.)

Ms. D: I love how put your story in a three-page booklet! Your story had a beginning, middle, and end. When you were reading your story out loud to me, I noticed that I couldn't follow some of the words. It seems like you had some trouble spelling some words that started with blends. I have the perfect writing tool for you!

(Ms. D takes out a blends chart and shows it to Timmy.)

Ms. D: Here's a blends chart for you to keep in your writing folder! When you're trying to write new words that you think may start with a blend, check this chart to help you figure out which blend to use. Look at the page where you wrote about the space shuttle blasting off. Let me look at the blends chart. Which word starts like the word *space*? Oh, I know…*sp*…*sp*…*spider*! That starts the same way. I could put that blend at the start of the word. Now you try it out with the word *blasting*.

Timmy: *Bl*…*bl*…*blocks*…oh…*blocks* starts the same way! I didn't write *bl* before!

(Timmy fixes his spelling.)

Ms. D: So the next time you're writing, remember to use this blends chart to help you.

(Ms. D hands him a "don't forget!" sticky note and places it on his writing piece. She then records the teaching on Timmy's conference note sheet so she can check up on how well he is using the tool during the next writing period.)

Using Your Assessments to Share Student Achievement Data With Parents

You can expect to meet with parents at least twice a year for parent-teacher conferences. However, you may meet with some parents more frequently if you are concerned about their children's writing. Conference note sheets help you remember specific skills the students are doing well with and those skills they need to improve on. Parents will be encouraged when you give them detailed compliments about their child's writing.

You may wish to take out each child's current unit Writing Conference Notes sheet for his or her parents to refer to during your conference. You might even photocopy your notes for them to take home. One quick glance at the objectives at the top, and parents can easily see how many objectives are checked and which ones students still need to achieve. Since the objectives are listed in order of difficulty, parents can get a clear picture of where their child is currently performing on the continuum of developing skills for writing workshop, as well as where he or she is headed.

For parent-teacher conferences, you can prepare a particular child's writing samples and the conference note sheets you've taken throughout the unit(s) to help guide your conversation. The dialogue below shows the skills that Ms. G, a kindergarten teacher, has been working on with Maria.

(Ms. G has set up a meeting with Maria's parents. She's meeting with them after school to discuss concerns about Maria's progress in writing workshop. Maria is having difficulties focusing during writing time and still does not follow the routines set in September. It's now November.)

Ms. G: Welcome. I really appreciate your coming. Maria is so lucky to have your support. Let's all sit down.

Maria's father: How's Maria doing?

Ms. G: Well, Maria really enjoys drawing. She does such beautiful illustrations. She's always eager to show me her work! Here are some of her proud pieces!

(Ms. G shows both parents Maria's writing samples.)

Ms. G: You can see she's a great illustrator. She writes about all kinds of things in her life—like Mom, skating, the park, her friends.

Maria's mother: She really likes to draw at home too!

Ms. G: I do want to share with you some concerns I have. I've been working with the class on routines for writing time. I confer with different students every day. All the children are supposed to sit down and write on their own while I'm talking to other children. Maria is so proud of her work that she keeps getting up to show me. I've communicated the workshop expectations during conferring time, and often reminded her to review these expectations before writing time, but problems persist. Let me show you my conference notes so you can get a better picture of what I'm talking about.

(Ms. G shows her notes to the family and explains what they mean. The first objective listed in the conference note sheet is that the writer understands and follows the routines of writing workshop. Ms. G points out that Maria is able to think of stories about her life to write about and can tell her story both orally and in writing. She needs to work on following the routines during conference time and to learn that a teacher's conference time with individual writers must not be interrupted.)

Maria's mother: We'll certainly talk to Maria about this behavior. We'll remind her that she needs to sit down and write more, and that there's always time to share at the end of the work-shop or at home with us. We appreciate your telling us about this.

Ms. G: Thanks so much. I'm sure the next time we meet I will have checked off objective A showing that Maria is fol-lowing all the rules. I'll be sure to give you an update in a week or so.

Our | Classroom Notes

We have found it very useful to show samples of a child's writing to his or her parents, who might not know what the standard for writing in that grade is. We always try to provide samples of writing by average writers in our classroom, and we make sure that the student's name is not shown. This helps us show parents the level of work we expect their child to do. We can then talk about ways to help their child progress at home.

Using Your Assessments to Share Student Achievement Data With Other Staff

You may need to meet periodically throughout the school year with some support staff to determine the best instructional program for students with special needs. Conference note sheets help you communicate your specific concerns to resource room teachers, literacy coaches, ESL teachers, academic intervention staff, speech teachers, and other colleagues. If all the teachers in your school choose to use the same conferring tools, the shared format and note-taking protocols will make communication easier and much more effective. By consulting the conference note sheets and reviewing objectives that children have made progress on and those they still need to work on, support staff can better help these writers when they work with students outside the classroom. They can also help you develop strategies that might help these children meet the objectives. For support staff such as instructional aides, who are not familiar with classroom expectations, these notes will help them better understand the big picture of the writing unit as well as the specific objectives individual children are working on.

Using the conference note sheets in mini-conferences with support staff, as shown below, makes it easy to collaborate and address students' key needs.

(Mr. J has set up a brief meeting with the ESL teacher, Ms. S, during their common prep period. He wants to update her on how the English language learners in his class are doing with regard to writing and to enlist her help so she can better support their writing during her pull-out instruction time.)

Mr. J: I just wanted to show you my conference note sheets for the students you work with. I know you sometimes work on writing with them, so I wanted to make sure you knew which goals I have this month for the second graders.

(Mr. J pulls out the conference note sheets and shows them to Ms. S. She reads them over.)

Ms. S: Oh, I didn't realize Bellal was still having difficulties with word endings. We've been working on that. I'll be sure to do some more word work to help him with this.

Mr. J: Great. That should help. Now, let's take a look at …

Using Your Assessments to Share Student Achievement Data With Administrators

In the course of the school year, there may also be times when you need to meet with your principal, assistant principal, or referral committee member to discuss students in your classroom you feel are at risk, and may need to receive additional services such as academic intervention, tutoring, or the resource room. It's important to have clear notes to show your administrators the areas of concern you have, as well as samples of student work. The more evidence you have, the more likely it is that your administration will be able to provide you and these students with the necessary support.

Occasionally you may need to refer these children for additional services. You can attach copies of your conference note sheets or Strategy Group Sheets to your referrals, in addition to student work samples, to provide evidence that the student is struggling despite the reteaching work that you've done. The following conversation is between a teacher and her principal:

(After school, Mrs. W meets with her principal, Mr. T, about Dylan's progress in first grade. It's midyear, and Dylan is still only drawing pictures with labels. He has trouble with letter-sound correspondence. When he's encouraged to write his story, he writes random strings of letters.)

Mrs. W: I wanted to talk with you about my student Dylan. He's been making very little progress. I was hoping he could begin to stay for extended day to get some help with writing.

Mr. T: What seems to be the problem?

Mrs. W: I brought my conference note sheets and some of Dylan's work to show you. (They look over Dylan's writing and the conference note sheets, and Mrs. W shows that Dylan has been working on using a picture alphabet chart as a strategy for spelling.)

Mr. T: I see that you've taught this lesson repeatedly, but Dylan hasn't been able to grasp the skill independently. How else do you think we could help him?

Mrs. W: I feel that Dylan could benefit from a small-group study on letter-sound recognition.

Mr. T: Let's send a note home right away about our extended day program.

Conferring is a powerful tool. It will help you get to know each student in your class as an individual learner. You will be able to say with great confidence what each student can and cannot do. It will guide you to better instruction for the whole-class, small groups, and one-on-one. When a teacher confers every day, the whole school community benefits. Conferring can help you create an ongoing support system that involves students, their parents, and school staff and administrators. Our goal is for every child to succeed, and conferring—when done consistently and purposefully—is an essential step toward reaching this goal.

References

PROFESSIONAL WORKS

Collins, Kathy. (2004). *Growing readers: Units of study in the primary classroom.* Portland, ME. Stenhouse Publishers.

Fletcher, Ralph. (1992). *What a writer needs.* Portsmouth, NH: Heinemann.

Fletcher, Ralph. (1999). *Live writing: Breathing life into your words.* New York: Avon Books.

Graves, Donald. (1994). *A fresh look at writing.* Portsmouth, NH: Heinemann.

Harwayne, Shelley. (1992). *Lasting impressions.* Portsmouth, NH: Heinemann.

Murray, Donald M. (2003). *A writer teaches writing.* Portsmouth, NH: Heinemann.

Portalupi, JoAnn and Fletcher, Ralph. (2001). *Writing workshop: The essential guide.* Portsmouth, NH: Heinemann.

Taberski, Sharon. (2000). *On solid ground: Strategies for teaching reading K–3.* Portsmouth, NH: Heinemann.

CHILDREN'S LITERATURE

Avery, Dorothy. (1998). *Black and white.* Chicago, IL: Shortland Publications, Inc.

Capucilli, Alyssa Satin. (1996). *Biscuit.* New York: HarperCollins Publishers.

Christelow, Eileen. (1995). *What do authors do?* New York: Clarion Books.

Feiffer, Jules. (2004). *The daddy mountain.* New York: Hyperion Books for Children.

Gamble, Danielle. (2004). *Poochie the poodle.* Chicago, IL: Wright Group/McGraw-Hill.

Gibbons, Gail. (1982). *The post office book: Mail and how it moves.* New York: HarperCollins Publishers.

Gibbons, Gail. (1984). *The seasons of Arnold's apple tree.* San Diego, CA: Voyager Books.

Graham, Bob. (2001). *"Let's get a pup!" said Kate.* Cambridge, MA: Candlewick Press.

Graham, Joan Bransfield. (1994). *Splish splash.* Boston: Houghton Mifflin Company.

Hess, Debra. (1994). *Wilson sat alone.* New York: Simon & Schuster Books for Young Readers.

Hesse, Karen. (1999). *Come on, rain!* New York: Scholastic Inc.

Hoberman, Mary Ann. (1991). *Fathers, mothers, sisters, brothers: A collection of family poems.* New York: Scholastic Inc.

Howe, James. (1990). *Pinky and Rex*. New York: Aladdin Paperbacks.

Keats, Ezra Jack. (1962). *The snowy day*. New York: Scholastic Inc.

Keats, Ezra Jack. (1977). *Whistle for Willie*. New York: Puffin Books.

London, Jonathan. (1985). *When the fireflies came*. New York: Aladdin Paperbacks.

O'Connor, Jane. (2006). *Fancy Nancy*. New York: HarperCollins Publishers.

Partridge, Elizabeth. (2003). *Whistling*. New York: Greenwillow Books.

Rylant, Cynthia. (1987). *Henry and Mudge*. New York: Aladdin Paperbacks.

Savadier, Elivia. (2005). *No haircut today!* Brookfield, CT: Roaring Book Press.

Smith, Christine. (1996). *Art smart: How to draw dinosaurs*. Milwaukee, WI: Gareth Stevens Publishing.

Spanyol, Jessica. (2001). *Carlo likes reading*. Cambridge, MA: Candlewick Press.

Tarpley, Natasha Anastasia. (1998). *I love my hair*. New York: Little Brown and Company.

Trussell-Cullen, Alan. (1998). *The whistle tooth*. Denver: Shortland Publications, Inc.

Weber, Rebecca. (1998). *Balcony garden*. Denver: Shortland Publications, Inc.

Whitcomb, Mary E. (1998). *Odd velvet*. San Francisco: Chronicle Books.

Wild, Margaret. (1993). *Our granny*. Boston: Houghton Mifflin Company.

Willems, Mo. (2004). *Knuffle bunny*. New York: Hyperion Books for Children.

Williams, Vera B. (1982). *A chair for my mother*. New York: Scholastic Inc.

Winstead, Rosie. (2006). *Ruby and Bubbles*. New York: Dial Books for Young Readers.

Yolen, Jane. (1987). *Owl moon*. New York: Scholastic, Inc.

Appendix: Reproducibles

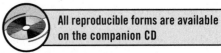

All reproducible forms are available on the companion CD

Tip

To customize and save the files on the CD, you will need to download Adobe Reader™, version 7.0 or higher. This download is available free of charge for Mac and PC systems at www.adobe.com/products/acrobat/readstep2.

Writing Conference Notes | Launching the Writing Workshop

UNIT OBJECTIVES

K–2 Developing Skills

A. Understands and follows the routines of writing workshop (conferring)
B. Generates ideas for writing topics
C. Is able to tell a story (orally and written)

D. Works cooperatively with a writing partner
E. Able to complete the writing process in a timely manner
F. Writes labels and/or sentences
G. Chooses appropriate paper

H. Uses sound-letter correspondence
I. Uses a variety of spelling strategies
J. Revises by adding to the pictures, adding words, or adding pages

Student: _____

Date/Text	What the Writer Can Do	Teaching Point	Next Steps

Writing Conference Notes | Many Kinds of Writing

UNIT OBJECTIVES

K–2 Developing Skills

A. Tries different kinds of writing
B. Uses different types of writing paper
C. Includes illustrations that go with the text

D. Rereads work with a partner
E. Accurately writes words from the word wall
F. Writes for an audience
G. Attempts to use punctuation appropriately

H. Uses consonant-vowel-consonant (cvc pattern) to spell words
I. Understands that writing is authentic and purposeful
J. Uses a style that matches the intended purpose of the piece

Student: _____

Date/Text	What the Writer Can Do	Teaching Point	Next Steps

 Differentiating Assessment in the Writing Workshop © 2008 by Karin Ma & Nicole Taylor, Scholastic Teaching Resources

Writing Conference Notes | Personal Narratives

Unit Objectives

A. Generates many story ideas about his or her life and writes (adequately)
B. Plans story effectively (uses strategies such as telling to a partner)
C. Follows publishing process (colors, adds title, creates cover)

D. Includes illustrations that are detailed and go with the text
E. Writes about a moment in his or her life
F. Uses initial and final consonants; uses high-frequency words
G. Stretches out one moment in a booklet format

H. Revises piece (e.g., adding more to heart of story, or main idea)
I. Edits (checks for and fixes errors in spelling, spacing, punctuation)
J. Uses a variety of spelling strategies

K–2 Developing Skills

Date/Text	What the Writer Can Do	Teaching Point	Next Steps

Student: _____

UNIT OBJECTIVES

K–2 Developing Skills

A. Writes about many small moments
B. Uses partner for support effectively; is a good writing partner
C. Follows the publishing process

D. Capitalizes the letter I
E. Uses neat, legible handwriting
F. Uses many spelling strategies (e.g., referring to word wall, chunks, alphabet chart, blends)
G. Uses consonant-vowel-consonant (cvc pattern) when writing

H. Rereads with an eye for editing (self-edits)
I. Writes with a consistent focus
J. Uses lowercase letters; capitalizes at beginning of a sentence

Student: _____

Date/Text	What the Writer Can Do	Teaching Point	Next Steps

Differentiating Assessment in the Writing Workshop © 2008 by Karin Ma & Nicole Taylor, Scholastic Teaching Resources

Writing Conference Notes | Revision

Unit Objectives

K–2 Developing Skills

A. Makes well-focused personal narratives (zooms in on the event)
B. Rereads independently to revise
C. Continues to use editing strategies from previous unit and prepares for publishing

D. Adds an interesting beginning and ending (e.g., weather, action)
E. Includes dialogue (speech bubbles and/or dialogue)
F. Uses a partner's help during the revision process
G. Writes in complete sentences

H. Uses revision tools effectively (e.g., caret insertions, revision strips)
I. Draws on multiple revision strategies
J. Revises in appropriate places

Student: _____

Date/Text	What the Writer Can Do	Teaching Point	Next Steps

UNIT OBJECTIVES

K–2 Developing Skills

A. Writes focused, interesting personal narratives (writes with rigor)
B. Reads like a writer (notices what published authors do)
C. Illustrates in the manner of a favorite author or illustrator

D. Uses revision strategies introduced in previous units
E. Creates a piece that is neat and easy to read
F. Writes an "about the author" page and dedication page
G. Uses an editing checklist

H. Edits a piece to match the style of a specific author
I. Uses many techniques learned during the study
J. Thinks about where to use author's crafts (chooses appropriate places)

Student: _____

Date/Text	What the Writer Can Do	Teaching Point	Next Steps

Differentiating Assessment in the Writing Workshop © 2008 by Karin Ma & Nicole Taylor, Scholastic Teaching Resources

Writing Conference Notes | Nonfiction: How To's

Unit Objectives

A. Makes appropriate topic choice (Asks: Have I done this before? Do I know how to do it?)
B. Plans out piece by acting it out
C. Tells steps sequentially

D. Uses time-order words and numbers
E. Includes materials section (picture glossary)
F. Adds diagrams with labels to clarify the steps
G. Rereads work with a partner and adds missing steps

H. Adds a strong introduction
I. Gives helpful advice or tips
J. Makes the steps elaborate and informative

K–2 Developing Skills

Student:

Date/Text	What the Writer Can Do	Teaching Point	Next Steps

Writing Conference Notes | Nonfiction: All About Books

UNIT OBJECTIVES

K–2 Developing Skills

A. Chooses a familiar topic (writer is an "expert")
B. Teaches the reader many useful facts about the topic
C. Chooses from a variety of types of paper; uses each appropriately

D. Includes nonfiction features
E. Uses vocabulary related to the topic and stays on topic
F. Edits using a checklist (spells important words right)
G. Works with a partner to improve a piece

H. Plans out and organizes topic (table of contents)
I. Writing is factual (fact vs. opinion)
J. Demonstrates understanding of narrative and nonnarrative text language

Date/Text	What the Writer Can Do	Teaching Point	Next Steps

Student: _____

Differentiating Assessment in the Writing Workshop © 2008 by Karin Ma & Nicole Taylor, Scholastic Teaching Resources

Writing Conference Notes | Poetry

Unit Objectives

K–2 Developing Skills

A. Writes various kinds of poems
B. Chooses topics from the heart
C. Composes poems that sound like poems (repetition)

D. Composes poems that sound like poems (rhythm, rhyme, beat)
E. Looks at things in unusual ways
F. Poems look like poems (white space)
G. Revises poems to create appropriate line breaks

H. Chooses poetic words (best language possible; most precise)
I. Revises poetry by discovering a new line to begin with
J. Communicates feelings through poetry

Student: _____

Date/Text	What the Writer Can Do	Teaching Point	Next Steps

Writing Conference Notes | Realistic Fiction

Unit Objectives

K–2 Developing Skills

A. Generates story ideas that are realistic
B. Writes longer stories
C. Works well with a writing partner

D. Develops reasonable solutions to the story conflict
E. Includes story elements
F. Writes stories with interesting, sophisticated problems
G. Edits thoroughly

H. Revises in many ways (e.g., adds dialogue and action)
I. Develops tension (e.g., character tries out solutions that don't work)
J. Creates and develops characters (uses names, traits, likes, and dislikes)

Date/Text	What the Writer Can Do	Teaching Point	Next Steps

Student: _____

Writing Conference Notes | For Unit _____ Month _____

UNIT OBJECTIVES _____

K–2 Developing Skills

A.
B.
C.

D.
E.
F.
G.

H.
I.
J.

Student: _____

Date/Text	What the Writer Can Do	Teaching Point	Next Steps

UNIT OBJECTIVES

K–2 Developing Skills

A. Understands and follows the routines of writing workshop (conferring)
B. Generates ideas for writing topics
C. Is able to tell a story (orally and written)

D. Works cooperatively with a writing partner
E. Able to complete the writing process in a timely manner
F. Writes labels and/or sentences
G. Chooses appropriate paper

H. Uses sound-letter correspondence
I. Uses a variety of spelling strategies
J. Revises by adding to the pictures, adding words, or adding pages

Students	A	B	C	D	E	F	G	H	I	J

Teacher: _____

Class: _____

• **Check off each objective when mastered or note date of mastery in box.**

Differentiating Assessment in the Writing Workshop © 2008 by Karin Ma & Nicole Taylor, Scholastic Teaching Resources

UNIT OBJECTIVES

A. Tries different kinds of writing
B. Uses different types of writing paper
C. Includes illustrations that go with the text

D. Rereads work with a partner
E. Accurately writes words from the word wall
F. Writes for an audience
G. Attempts to use punctuation appropriately

H. Uses consonant-vowel-consonant (cvc pattern) to spell words
I. Understands that writing is authentic and purposeful
J. Uses a style that matches the intended purpose of the piece

K–2 Developing Skills

Students	A	B	C	D	E	F	G	H	I	J

Teacher: _____

Class: _____

• **Check off each objective when mastered or note date of mastery in box.**

Differentiating Assessment in the Writing Workshop © 2008 by Karin Ma & Nicole Taylor, Scholastic Teaching Resources

Class Checklist | Personal Narratives

UNIT OBJECTIVES

A. Generates many story ideas about his or her life and writes (adequately)
B. Plans story effectively (uses strategies such as telling to a partner)
C. Follows publishing process (colors, adds title, creates cover)

D. Includes illustrations that are detailed and go with the text
E. Writes about a moment in his or her life
F. Uses initial and final consonants; uses high-frequency words
G. Stretches out one moment in a booklet format

H. Revises piece (e.g., adding more to heart of story, or main idea)
I. Edits (checks for and fixes errors in spelling, spacing, punctuation)
J. Uses a variety of spelling strategies

K–2 Developing Skills

Students	A	B	C	D	E	F	G	H	I	J

Teacher: _____

Class: _____

• **Check off each objective when mastered or note date of mastery in box.**

Differentiating Assessment in the Writing Workshop © 2008 by Karin Ma & Nicole Taylor, Scholastic Teaching Resources

Class Checklist | Writing for Readers

UNIT OBJECTIVES

K–2 Developing Skills

A. Writes about many small moments
B. Uses partner for support effectively; is a good writing partner
C. Follows the publishing process

D. Capitalizes the letter I
E. Uses neat, legible handwriting
F. Uses many spelling strategies (e.g., referring to word wall, chunks, alphabet chart, blends)
G. Uses consonant-vowel-consonant (cvc pattern) when writing

H. Rereads with an eye for editing (self-edits)
I. Writes with a consistent focus
J. Uses lowercase letters; capitalizes at beginning of a sentence

Students	A	B	C	D	E	F	G	H	I	J

Teacher: _____

Class: _____

• **Check off each objective when mastered or note date of mastery in box.**

Differentiating Assessment in the Writing Workshop © 2008 by Karin Ma & Nicole Taylor, Scholastic Teaching Resources

Class Checklist | Revision

Class Checklist | Revision

Unit Objectives

K–2 Developing Skills

A. Makes well-focused personal narratives (zooms in on the event)
B. Rereads independently to revise
C. Continues to use editing strategies from previous unit and prepares for publishing

D. Adds an interesting beginning and ending (e.g., weather, action)
E. Includes dialogue (speech bubbles and/or dialogue)
F. Uses a partner's help during the revision process
G. Writes in complete sentences

H. Uses revision tools effectively (e.g., caret insertions, revision strips)
I. Draws on multiple revision strategies
J. Revises in appropriate places

Teacher: _____

Class: _____

Students	A	B	C	D	E	F	G	H	I	J

• **Check off each objective when mastered or note date of mastery in box.**

Class Checklist | Author's Craft Study

UNIT OBJECTIVES

K–2 Developing Skills

A. Writes focused, interesting personal narratives (writes with rigor)
B. Reads like a writer (notices what published authors do)
C. Illustrates in the manner of a favorite author or illustrator

D. Uses revision strategies introduced in previous units
E. Creates a piece that is neat and easy to read
F. Writes an "about the author" page and dedication page
G. Uses an editing checklist

H. Edits a piece to match the style of a specific author
I. Uses many techniques learned during the study
J. Thinks about where to use author's crafts (chooses appropriate places)

Students	A	B	C	D	E	F	G	H	I	J

Teacher: _____

Class: _____

• **Check off each objective when mastered or note date of mastery in box.**

Differentiating Assessment in the Writing Workshop © 2008 by Karin Ma & Nicole Taylor, Scholastic Teaching Resources

Class Checklist | Nonfiction: How To's

UNIT OBJECTIVES

K–2 Developing Skills

A. Makes appropriate topic choice (Asks: Have I done this before? Do I know how to do it?)
B. Plans out piece by acting it out
C. Tells steps sequentially

D. Uses time-order words and numbers
E. Includes materials section (picture glossary)
F. Adds diagrams with labels to clarify the steps
G. Rereads work with a partner and adds missing steps

H. Adds a strong introduction
I. Gives helpful advice or tips
J. Makes the steps elaborate and informative

Students	A	B	C	D	E	F	G	H	I	J

Teacher: _____

Class: _____

• **Check off each objective when mastered or note date of mastery in box.**

Differentiating Assessment in the Writing Workshop © 2008 by Karin Ma & Nicole Taylor, Scholastic Teaching Resources

Class Checklist | Nonfiction: All About Books

UNIT OBJECTIVES

K–2 Developing Skills

A. Chooses a familiar topic (writer is an "expert")
B. Teaches the reader many useful facts about the topic
C. Chooses from a variety of types of paper; uses each appropriately

D. Includes nonfiction features
E. Uses vocabulary related to the topic and stays on topic
F. Edits using a checklist (spells important words right)
G. Works with a partner to improve a piece

H. Plans out and organizes topic (table of contents)
I. Writing is factual (fact vs. opinion)
J. Demonstrates understanding of narrative and nonnarrative text language

Students	A	B	C	D	E	F	G	H	I	J

Teacher: _____

Class: _____

• **Check off each objective when mastered or note date of mastery in box.**

Class Checklist | Poetry

UNIT OBJECTIVES

K–2 Developing Skills

A. Writes various kinds of poems
B. Chooses topics from the heart
C. Composes poems that sound like poems (repetition)

D. Composes poems that sound like poems (rhythm, rhyme, beat)
E. Looks at things in unusual ways
F. Poems look like poems (white space)
G. Revises poems to create appropriate line breaks

H. Chooses poetic words (best language possible; most precise)
I. Revises poetry by discovering a new line to begin with
J. Communicates feelings through poetry

Students	A	B	C	D	E	F	G	H	I	J

Teacher: _____

Class: _____

• **Check off each objective when mastered or note date of mastery in box.**

UNIT OBJECTIVES

K–2 Developing Skills

A. Generates story ideas that are realistic
B. Writes longer stories
C. Works well with a writing partner

D. Develops reasonable solutions to the story conflict
E. Includes story elements
F. Writes stories with interesting, sophisticated problems
G. Edits thoroughly

H. Revises in many ways (e.g., adds dialogue and action)
I. Develops tension (e.g., character tries out solutions that don't work)
J. Creates and develops characters (uses names, traits, likes, and dislikes)

Students	A	B	C	D	E	F	G	H	I	J

Teacher: _____

Class: _____

• **Check off each objective when mastered or note date of mastery in box.**

Differentiating Assessment in the Writing Workshop © 2008 by Karin Ma & Nicole Taylor, Scholastic Teaching Resources

Class Checklist | For Unit _____ Month _____

UNIT OBJECTIVES _____

K–2 Developing Skills

- A.
- B.
- C. _____

- D.
- E.
- F.
- G. _____

- H.
- I.
- J.

Students	A	B	C	D	E	F	G	H	I	J

Teacher: _____

Class: _____

- **Check off each objective when mastered or note date of mastery in box.**

 Differentiating Assessment in the Writing Workshop © 2008 by Karin Ma & Nicole Taylor, Scholastic Teaching Resources

For Unit _____ Month _____

Students	◀——————— Conference Dates ———————▶				

Teacher: _____

Class: _____

Planning Form | Planning a Unit

Previous Unit of Study: _____ Month: _____

What Went Well	Reflections	Work to Continue in the Unit

Current Unit of Study: _____ Month: _____

Writing Objectives	Teaching Points

Upcoming Unit of Study: _____ Month: _____

Writing Objectives	Teaching Points

Differentiating Assessment in the Writing Workshop © 2008 by Karin Ma & Nicole Taylor, Scholastic Teaching Resources

Planning Form | Planning a Mini-Lesson

Unit of Study _____ Month _____

Unit Objective _____

Teaching Point _____

ACTIVATING PRIOR KNOWLEDGE

How will you connect to your teaching point?

❏ Students   ❏ Books   ❏ Previous Lessons

PRESENTING YOUR TEACHING POINT

How will you do it?

❏ Demonstrate   ❏ Fishbowl   ❏ Texts

ACHIEVING ACTIVE ENGAGEMENT

How will students practice?

❏ Charts   ❏ Student Work   ❏ Turn & Talk   ❏ Act It Out

Planning Form | Strategy Group Sheet

Writing Unit: _____

Teacher: _____

Class: _____

Date: _____

Unit Objective: _____

Specific Skill: _____

_____

Tools Used: _____

Students:

❑ 1. _____

❑ 2. _____

❑ 3. _____

❑ 4. _____

❑ 5. _____

Notes: _____

_____

Date: _____

Unit Objective: _____

Specific Skill: _____

_____

Tools Used: _____

Students:

❑ 1. _____

❑ 2. _____

❑ 3. _____

❑ 4. _____

❑ 5. _____

Notes: _____

_____

Date: _____

Unit Objective: _____

Specific Skill: _____

_____

Tools Used: _____

Students:

❑ 1. _____

❑ 2. _____

❑ 3. _____

❑ 4. _____

❑ 5. _____

Notes: _____

_____

Date: _____

Unit Objective: _____

Specific Skill: _____

_____

Tools Used: _____

Students:

❑ 1. _____

❑ 2. _____

❑ 3. _____

❑ 4. _____

❑ 5. _____

Notes: _____

_____

Differentiating Assessment in the Writing Workshop © 2008 by Karin Ma & Nicole Taylor, Scholastic Teaching Resources

Meet Our Writers

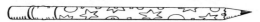

Name: _____ Date: _____

1. Do you like to write?

   Yes 😊 _____   No ☹ _____

2. When do you like to write?

   Morning _____   Noon _____   Night _____

3. Where do you like to write?

   Home _____   School _____   Other ? _____

4. What do you like to write about?

   _____

   _____

   _____

5. Why?

   _____

   _____

Meet Our Writers

Name: _____ Date: _____

1. Do you like to write? What do you like to write about?

_____

_____

2. When do you write? Where do you write?

_____

_____

3. When you have trouble writing a word, what do you do?

_____

_____

4. What about writing is easy for you?

_____

_____

5. What about writing is hard for you?

_____

_____

6. Why do people write?

_____

_____

You Are Invited!

To: _____

From: _____

What? _____

Why? _____

When? _____

Where? _____

Please respond by _____

✂ -

Cut and return the bottom slip to_____, room _____.
Thank you!

Your name: _____

Author who invited you: _____

❑ Yes, I am excited about coming!   ☺

❑ Sorry I can't make it! Thank you!   ☹

Something I plan to bring: _____

Differentiating Assessment in the Writing Workshop © 2008 by Karin Ma & Nicole Taylor, Scholastic Teaching Resources

✩ ✩ **Celebration Comment Sheet** ✩ ✩

Author: _____

Date: _____

Title: _____

_____

Thank you for coming to my celebration!

What did you think about my piece?

Comments:
Name: _____
Name: _____
Name: _____
Name: _____

Name: _____ Date: _____

Name: _____ Date: _____

Differentiating Assessment in the Writing Workshop © 2008 by Karin Ma & Nicole Taylor, Scholastic Teaching Resources

Name: _____ Date: _____

Name: _____ Date: _____

Picture Glossary of _____

```
┌─────────────────────────────────────────────────────┐
│                                                     │
│                                                     │
│                                                     │
│                                                     │
│                                                     │
│                                                     │
│                                                     │
│                                                     │
│                                                     │
│                                                     │
│                                                     │
│                                                     │
│                                                     │
│                                                     │
│                                                     │
└─────────────────────────────────────────────────────┘
```

_____   _____

_____   _____

_____   _____

Name: _____ Date: _____

Questions and Answers About _____

Question 1:

Answer 1:

Question 2:

Answer 2:

Name: _____ Date: _____

Important Words About _____

_____

_____

_____

_____

_____

_____

_____

_____

Name: _____ Date: _____

What's On My Mind?

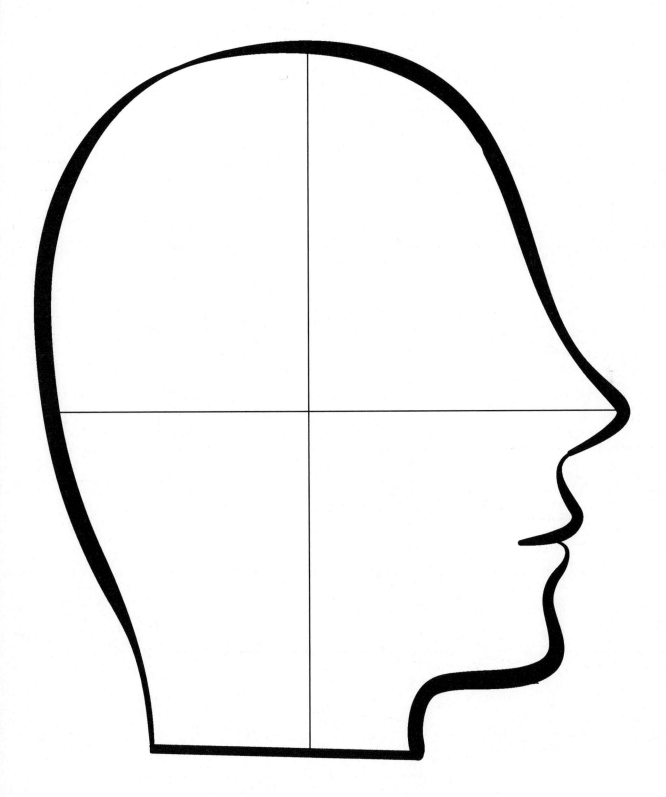

Index